Sales Mastery Essentials Made Simple

SALES MASTERY
Essentials
MADE SIMPLE

**YOUR MASTER CLASS ON SELLING
WITH 7 KEYS TO BECOMING A
SALES MACHINE**

RUTH M. FARRINGTON

NEW YORK

LONDON • NASHVILLE • MELBOURNE • VANCOUVER

Sales Mastery Essentials Made Simple

Your Master Class on Selling with 7 Keys to Becoming a Sales Machine

Published in New York, New York, by Morgan James Publishing. Morgan James is a trademark of Morgan James, LLC. www.MorganJamesPublishing.com

Proudly distributed by Publishers Group West®

Morgan James BOGO™

A **FREE** ebook edition is available for you or a friend with the purchase of this print book.

CLEARLY SIGN YOUR NAME ABOVE

Instructions to claim your free ebook edition:
1. Visit MorganJamesBOGO.com
2. Sign your name CLEARLY in the space above
3. Complete the form and submit a photo of this entire page
4. You or your friend can download the ebook to your preferred device

ISBN 9781636982502 paperback
ISBN 9781636982519 ebook
Library of Congress Control Number:
202393719

Cover Design by:
Chris Treccani
www.3dogcreative.net

Interior Design by:
Christopher Kirk
www.GFSstudio.com

Morgan James is a proud partner of Habitat for Humanity Peninsula and Greater Williamsburg. Partners in building since 2006.

Get involved today! Visit: www.morgan-james-publishing.com/giving-back

This book is dedicated to my mother, my first teacher, my biggest fan, and the one who helped me get started with everything in life, especially the extraordinary career I have been enjoying in sales.

TABLE OF CONTENTS

ACKNOWLEDGMENTS

I have been deeply fortunate to have worked with many great companies and mentors who helped shape, mold, and influence everything I am and know. I thank all of them for placing me in the front row seat of the engine that drives the world's economy and professional sales.

I also want to thank all the wonderful people I have been honored to serve and work with throughout my career. Especially those who have made up some of the best sales teams I've ever witnessed in action. They know who they are. When you're on a sales team that's performing at the peak of its ability every single day, you feel it right down to the bottom of your comfortable shoes. You feel how special that is. It's a feeling you need to grab hold of for as long as you possibly can because it is sweet but fleeting.

I want to thank my family and all of my dear friends, especially my three sons, Michael, Tyler, and Kyle. I was not always there for them the way they wanted me to be sometimes. All the same, everything I have done since they were born, I have been doing with all the love in my heart for them.

I would like to thank Morgan James Publishing and the phenomenal team that helped to make my dream of writing this book a reality. And last, but certainly not least, I would like to thank Dr. George W. Jackson, Jr., my companion, my light, my silent partner, for the advice, inspiration, and support he's given me throughout this incredible authorship journey.

PREFACE

In my life, I've delivered untold hundreds of thousands of sales presentations in a spirit of consummate professionalism, enthusiasm, and joy. I've been responsible for closing over a half million sales. What is more, I've been responsible for over $5 billion in retail and wholesale sales revenue over the past 48 years for the companies I've served. I've trained and touched the lives of thousands of sales representatives. I've traveled extensively throughout the U.S. and internationally while managing a thriving household and raising three exceptional sons.

Like many Baby Boomers, I am entering a third phase or a third wave in my life.

The first wave was getting myself established. I feel like I was a master at sales long before I went pro. Once I started working in sales at 16, I bought my car. I bought lots of clothes. Yeah, I managed to save a bit but shared a lot of it. If somebody needed money, my sister, brother, or friends, they already knew I made a lot of money, and I was a much softer touch than my parents. So, they came at me and came at me, and I just handed money out like it was candy. But it made me happy. I didn't mind. I was making what would be, in today's dollars, about $15,000 per year, and I wasn't even 18 years old, and I was only working part-time. My mother couldn't believe it.

The Second Wave was chasing the American Dream. I married, raised a family, and kept scaling up homes until I could afford my dream home. I still had plenty of clothes, luxury cars—all because of work. I also continued scaling up my career, going from retail and business management at the age of 17 to being a buyer at age 23, then a wholesale national showroom manager, to being a national sales manager as well as district manager for several well-known luxury brands. In fact. I've spent most of my career in luxury brands, affluent clientele, high-ticket items, concierge services, and high commissions and bonuses. The second wave afforded me an excellent living but not without a lot of sacrifices.

Now, in my third wave, the emphasis is on giving something back. Instead of taking all of this hard-fought and hard-won experience quietly to the grave, I now can take this experience and distill it into its essence—the essentials. This is my story, and with a little effort and attention, this will be your story, too—even bigger and better than I ever dreamed. Here's to you.

INTRODUCTION

Devote today to something so daring
even you can't believe you're doing it.
Oprah Winfrey

've been selling since I was 16. As of this writing, I am 64 and would argue that I was a master of selling long before I took my first paid sales gig. All the same, I have five decades of mastery from small-ticket to large-ticket luxury retail. Over five decades, I've excelled in every position, from floor rep and floor manager to district manager, showroom manager, and national sales manager. I've also worked at all ends of the retail industry, including wholesaling and whole-sale management and dealing with national and international supply chains.

You can say sales is a skill, and skill is essential. You can say selling is an art. Whether you see yourself as creative or not, a sale is always created in the client's mind before they ever sign on the dotted line or e-sign, DocuSign, scribble on a signature pad, whatever, you get the point.

You can say selling is a passion. I will hold out that mastery of sales absolutely requires passion. Many people might say it's a passion for money. I don't necessarily think so, as a passion for money alone isn't going to make you a master of the game. To achieve mastery in a field that, by its nature, is built around serving the client's needs, there has to be a passion deep inside for making someone else's life better.

If you are genuinely making someone else's life better, in a meaningful way, no matter how small, you are also making your life better, and that, my friend, deserves a celebration at all times.

Sales gets a bad rap because bad sales tactics have been used since the beginning of time and are still being used to cheat people, sometimes out of millions. Let's face it, feeling like you've been cheated out of even one dollar is enough to make most people very annoyed at the very least. And if you're like me, you'll get all-out pissed. Cheating is dishonest and unfair. No human deserves to be treated that way. We know that pretty much from the time we can understand anything about life. I submit that if a sale (no matter how small) does not result in a celebration (no matter how small), then someone has been cheated. Cheating is a form of robbery.

I don't think I'm exaggerating to say that honoring the very essence of life is something sacred, or at least it should be treated that way. The transfer of value and service from one human being to another is the essence of life. To truly master selling, be it low ticket, high ticket, business to consumer, business to business, complex, multi-stage, proposal based, sophisticated high-tech selling, right down to a kid's sidewalk lemonade stand, to make someone else's life better, whether it's millions of people or just one person, is a high calling. To know that puts you on the road to success in any endeavor. To live that way puts you on the road to mastery.

> The transfer of value and service from one human being to another is the essence of life.

What you will find inside this book is your pathway to sales mastery. This pathway will allow you to prosper in every way imaginable and bring prosperity to everyone you love as well as people you don't even know and may never meet. This mastery can be applied to any situation, industry, market, or economic environment.

What you have right now in your hand—or on some electronic screen—will give you the keys to earning a high income for a lifetime. All it requires you to do is elevate your understanding of why. The why behind the sale, in every situation, is to bring about and savor a cause for celebration.

The voyage you are about to embark on will take you through a 7-step process that is universal, time-tested, and proven to work. This process has been stripped down to its bare simplicity. I can summarize it for you in three words: see, solve, and satisfy. Let's go ahead now and dive in.

THE S³ METHOD IN A NUTSHELL

With the see-solve-satisfy (S³) method, my goal is to take something as complex and intricate as professional selling and break it down into its fundamental strategies and components. From that point, we can focus on the essential qualities that solidify your ascendance into sales mastery or accelerate the level of mastery you already have.

S³ METHOD OVERVIEW

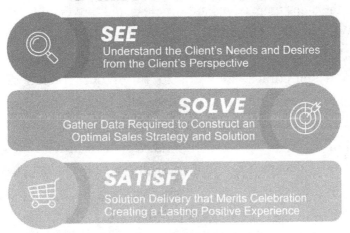

SEE
Understand the Client's Needs and Desires from the Client's Perspective

SOLVE
Gather Data Required to Construct an Optimal Sales Strategy and Solution

SATISFY
Solution Delivery that Merits Celebration Creating a Lasting Positive Experience

Figure 1. The See, Solve, Satisfy S3 Method Summarized

The heart and soul of any sales transaction is to fill a client's need and engage in an exchange of value. Between the two, there is usually a puzzle to be solved. In some cases, maybe even many cases, the puzzle is so well-known, like *Tic-Tac-Toe*, the puzzle does not offer significant challenges. Stated another way, the difference between a successful sale and no sale always lies in the solution to the puzzle.

I like to think of sales as a jigsaw puzzle. Maybe not the 40,000-piece *Memorable Disney Moments* jigsaw puzzle that was confirmed by the Guinness World Records as the largest commercially made puzzle in the world, both in the number of pieces and its overall size. Once your sales puzzle is completed, it needs to present and fulfill a picture in your client's mind that's as beautiful as any scene from a Walt Disney animated film.

To accomplish this, there are prodigious steps to be taken, to be sure. While the time and intensity dedicated to each step may vary, the steps themselves are timeless and universal.

We obviously have to engage our clients in some way, and that engagement takes place around our client's desires. Though sometimes, in order to fulfill our client's deepest wishes and arrive at an outcome that results in a sale, we have to gain information that might only be given after a certain level of trust has been established. Connection with the client is how and where we begin earning the level of trust that allows us to explore the client's past, current, and future situations with an increasing depth that allows us to design and describe a future that the client must agree will leave them much better off after they've adopted our solution rather than any other option.

SEVEN COMPONENTS
OF THE S³ METHOD

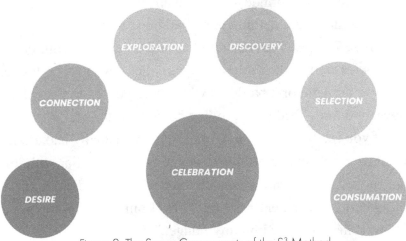

Figure 2. The Seven Components of the S³ Method

The client's recognition or discovery that we've designed and described their ideal solution is the goal of the discovery phase. This is where the client discovers that our solution not only exceeds all their expectations, but they can also satisfy all of their wishes at an exceedingly favorable value. The value must be so heavily weighted in their favor (logically and emotionally) that they cannot help but make a selection in your favor, provided they are being fair, honest, and forthcoming.

> *The client's recognition or discovery that we've designed and described their ideal solution is the goal of the discovery phase.*

Let's face it, there will always be tire-kickers, window shoppers, and people with nothing better to do than to waste their and your time. We're talking about helping the clients who really do need your help. Everyone else we can let go of as soon as possible. As long as you reach inside for the very best at every opportunity, you continue to sharpen and hone your skills for the next encounter, and nothing is wasted on your part.

These 7 steps, when mastered, create a change in your entire outlook as well as the outlook of your client. Sales is no longer a power struggle or a battle of wits where you must tie a client down and force-feed your product down their throat.

If you can believe it, back in the day, we actually had a sales technique we called a tie-down. If you are not familiar with this technique, a tie-down was where you positioned a client to make or agree to a statement such as, "Yes, I am ready to buy a car today, if the price is within my budget."

Then, once you've cornered your prey in the verbal lion's den of your well-trained closing strategy, the client was supposedly tied down by the fact they had earlier said they would buy today if it were in their budget.

It went something like, "But, Mr. Smith, you told me $100 per month was in your budget, right? Were you lying to me then or are you lying to me now? You're not really a liar, are you, Mr. Smith?

I was brought up to believe the only thing lower than a liar was someone who'd steal their grandmother's false teeth and help her look for them after he sold them for the gold. You wouldn't do anything like that now, would you, Mr. Smith? I thought not. Here you go, just sign on the dotted line, right here, here, here, and initial there. Thank you."

Times have changed. In today's world, consumers of just about anything and everything have so many options and alternatives (they walk through the door knowing about or knowing other options are only a Google search away) that the key to sales mastery in modern times is to come together with clients as equal partners in terms of knowledge. Equal partners work together in the very best interest of the client—first, foremost, and always. This is our mantra. This is our highway to mastery. This creates engagements leading to consummation rather than closing. Once the required groundwork is well-executed, closing is a foregone conclusion leading to the place where selling becomes a celebration.

SEE THE INVISIBLE

Chapter 1

ASSESS THEIR HIDDEN DESIRES

I have a deeply hidden and inarticulate desire
for something beyond the daily life.
Virginia Woolf

I did a bad, bad thing when I was 16. I got myself a job. It was at a Detroit-based retail store in my hometown of Cleveland, Ohio, named Winkelman's. This was one of my mom's favorite places to shop for clothing, and she was a frequent customer. The store was very refined, relatively upscale, and extremely open and friendly. My mother was in the fitting room trying on something classy and sophisticated as usual. It was late September at the time. I had just started high school. I was nearly a straight-A student, yet I often had a lot of time on my hands. Lots of time on your hands could be a problem for a teenage girl surrounded by teenage boys slathered with uncontrollable hormones. Anyway, I took it upon myself to go after the store manager and ask her if she might be hiring for seasonal work.

I don't know why I did it. I only remember watching a young girl, not much older than I was, working the floor and thinking, *I can do that.*

Mrs. Russell, the store manager, smiled with what I think was a little admiration and said she certainly did have openings for seasonal work. While my mom was still in there trying on clothing, she had no idea her 16-year-old baby girl was on the lower level of the store filling out a job application.

Now you must understand that my mom was from New Orleans and could be as fiery as homemade Louisiana hot sauce. She was also a gorgeous woman and highly protective of all her kids. I've also had asthma all my life, and I spent most of my life, other than school and church, shuttered away indoors. This was because I was practically allergic to everything airborne. Well, maybe not everything—but a lot.

Well, to my surprise, when mom did find out I had applied for a job, she was more shocked than livid (and some category of livid was what I was expecting). She tried to explain to me I was too young. She tried to explain to me that she didn't see or understand how I would be able to do that sort of job, what with all my studies and chores to keep up with. And in addition to all of that, I had no sales experience whatsoever. She had a point. Heck, I didn't even know how I would do all of that either. Still, something inside me said, *You can do this.*

Mrs. Russell knew my mother was an excellent customer. My mother seldom left Winkelman's without enough bags for both of us to carry. Mrs. Russell assured my mom she would look out for me as if I were her own; by some miracle, my mom agreed. So, the deal was struck, and I worked at Winkelman's from Thanksgiving until January 1.

Tracing a little bit of my roots one more time, not the roots when I need my hair touched up, but the roots of my familial love for fashion, my mother and my grandmother both had an all-out knack for looking great and dressing even better. My mother was feisty as all get out, but at the same time she was a revertant churchgoing woman. They do grow 'em like that down in Louisiana. If she could, I am sure my mother would have had a different hat for every Sunday of the year. She kept a couple of dozen hats around all the time, which was a good start.

My grandmother, Mama Ruth, was a seamstress for Steven's Specialty Store near the Terminal Tower in Cleveland. Even with modest means, Mama Ruth could dress like a million bucks. She was always flawlessly attired. She probably gave fashion advice to St. Peter at the Gates of Heaven. I can see her saying, "I can help you do something with that robe, you know."

Both mom and Mama Ruth demonstrated that you don't have to spend a lot to look radiant at any time, but you do have to pay scrupulous attention to every detail of your look. Fashion is a massive part of my story. My love for fashion started early in life and remains with me to this day.

All the same, my fashion sense led to my first mistake as a newly minted retail sales rep. On my first day, I wore a fabulous pair of "dress to kill" shoes. Oh, there was a killing, all right. Halfway through the shift, my feet said, "It's them or us, Honey. Take your pick."

So, on my first day in sales, I spent more time standing behind the counter in my bare feet than walking the floor talking to customers. I learned my first lesson in professional sales: If you're going to be on your feet all day, you'll need comfortable shoes or a podiatrist.

Nevertheless, as I was saying, at a very early age, I learned volumes of data about how women look at clothing and accessories and how they influence how women look at the world and, most importantly, how they look at themselves. Looking back now, I can see how I translated everything I'd ever learned up to that point into the retail sales experience. I learned to sell the hell out of women's clothing and accessories. Not only that, I studied and learned from the other sales associates incessantly over time, but initially, I flew on gut instinct and a lot of moxie.

Looking back at my early years, I knew without anyone telling me that a woman's scarf was not simply a scarf. I could see that a scarf could be a Monet landscape painted gently around a woman's neck, helping her see and feel that it made the rest of her outfit go together so well she could not possibly leave the store without it. I knew that jewelry was not simply a trinket, even costume jewelry—no, no, no, no, no. I had to see who the person thought they would be when they wore that piece of jewelry. Then if I could gently re-enforce and even subtly acknowledge who that new person was, that new person walked out of the store with a purchase.

I learned through the world of fashion that everyone has deep desires they may not ever articulate, but if you can find them and put your finger on the pulse of a deeply hidden desire, its beat will lead you to help them in the best way possible. Sometimes the best way, to be honest, is no sale at all. On the other hand, when the best way to help them turns out to be a purchase (the bigger, the better, of course), you help them make that purchase, but you also make them feel good about the purchase they just made. As a result, they smile and thank you for helping them make a purchase that just put money in your pocket. What's not to love about that?

Armed with that knowledge and incentive, though purely instinctive at the time, I was raking in cash like I'd stolen a printing press from the U.S. Treasury.

Maslow's Hierarchy Is Only a Starting Point

Nobody likes to be sold. In fact, in our mega-chaotic, endless sales messaging, modern world, people of all ages loathe the idea of being sold. Just hitting up Google a minute ago tells me the average person is exposed to something like 5,000 ads per day. Of course, we don't see or pay any attention to 5,000 ads per day; I mean, how could we? But I don't doubt there are at least that many sales messages out there every day. Like, I don't doubt that there's a piece of lint in one of my pockets right now. We all know we spend most of our waking hours being bombarded with messages to buy, buy, buy, or else, eat, eat, eat, eat. Or better yet, buy something to eat now, now, now, now, now. And the list goes on.

Since we are still at the beginning of our story, and there's ample time for me to take it all back later, I want to take you on a slight detour for the next couple of pages. I want to do this now to draw your attention to what some of you may find to be a startling distinction I am making between sales and marketing for the sake of this book.

Attention, interest, desire, and action (AIDA) is a well-known sales and advertising formula. For this book, capturing attention and interest, at least initially, is a matter of marketing. In my experience, actual selling always begins and ends with desire.

The way I am seeing it, there was a time when selling alone ruled the day, long before 1440, when mass printing and publication were enabled by Gutenberg and his printing press, and long before 1796, when lithography was invented, making it possible to put up sales posters all over town.

Indeed, advertising grew as advertising media evolved. With the invention of the radio and, later on, television, mass market advertising began to rule the day. Most of the salesforce increasingly became order takers as clients were often already sold on the product before showing up at your door.

At that point, most of your clients only needed guidance on pricing, selection, and delivery. For those industries that still required someone to go out and "press the flesh" to close the deal and make the sale, of which there were still many, genuine sales professionals still showed up with briefcases and calling cards in hand, along with one or two entertaining stories to tell.

As our society aged and its people became savvier and more sophisticated, the power of advertising all by itself began to attenuate. Moreover, the Baby Boom created a surge of consumer buying power, and our capitalistic society responded with competition (wherever it was not crushed and snuffed out by a monopoly).

The need for increased sales skills and sales expertise, which had never gone away, became more prominent. Likewise, books about professional selling tools and techniques began to proliferate.

While marketing has been practiced for thousands of years, don't get me wrong, and college-level courses in marketing have been taught since the early 1900s, I recall the word *marketing* coming into mainstream conversations in the 1970s.

Once again, don't get me wrong, as advertising is a function of marketing, to be sure. Still, it became more and more apparent that in commerce, whether it be mass or local, the ability to capture the attention and interest of the consumer changed dramatically as the nature of society changed.

As the whole of selling has its own unique universe of challenges, it became increasingly incumbent upon marketing to analyze, understand, and translate changes in an evolving marketplace to facilitate and optimize the environment in which a sale can be made.

Part of the value of participating in sales for almost half a century is that I've watched firsthand as marketing has grown in prominence and stature to the point where the chief marketing officer, in many cases, is just as indispensable as the chief sales officer.

So, I am saying all this because you might be thinking, *What about sales prospecting? What about sales lead generation?* Obviously, customer acquisition is vital, but gone are the days when you can expect a sales professional to bang out 1,000 cold calls in the morning and then go out and close a couple of dozen sales by the end of the day.

There has been a seismic shift in the customer acquisition business model. Today's prospective clients have more features and pricing data, more access to alternative options and, in some cases, more knowledge about a particular product in your product line than you do. Modern customer acquisition, if it is to be done thoughtfully, requires taking into account the entire customer journey and leading prospective clients into a sort of funnel. There are zillions of those from what I can tell. What I do know is that ideally, you want that funnel to resemble a black hole where once a client crosses the event horizon, they are sucked in for good. But the old days of yanking customers off the street, shoving them into a chair, and browbeating them until they bought something or called the police, is a model that no longer has a remote chance of success.

That is primarily because I would say the average 13-year-old today is more sophisticated, in every way, than the average 21-year-old in the 1950s and maybe even the 1960s. With that leap in the worldliness and skepticism of our younger generations, which can only increase over time, we already know that our attempts to capture attention and interest are doomed to remain a never-ending battle. Fortunately for me, and probably you, too, I'm not writing about that. When it comes to selling, our game begins with desire.

This concludes our detour, and we're returning to the original point. We begin with you in front of the client, in the first stage of our process, engaging the client's desires and seeing if you can find clues on what will motivate them to buy after all is said and done.

Maslow's hierarchy of needs is a theory in psychology that suggests that there are specific needs that individuals must satisfy to reach their full potential. According to Maslow, these needs can be divided into five categories: physiological, safety, love/belonging, esteem, and self-actualization. While some may quibble with Maslow or offer different points of view, let's stick with this paradigm for the moment as it has stood up to the test of time.

Maslow's Hierarchy of Needs

Figure 3. Maslow is only a starting point in your search for buying motives

Physiological needs are individuals' most basic needs to satisfy in order to survive. This includes needs such as food, water, shelter, and clothing. Safety needs are the next needs, including security and protection from harm. Love/belonging needs are social needs that help us feel connected to others and include things like friendship and intimacy. Esteem needs are about feeling good about ourselves and include self-respect and achievement. Finally, self-actualization needs are about reaching our full potential as individuals and can include creativity and personal growth.

Maslow's hierarchy of needs is only a starting point when attempting to assess human motivation for any reason and certainly when we are looking for a client's buried treasures—their hidden desires.

Many other factors can affect someone's motivation, and it's necessary to consider them when trying to understand why someone may or may not engage in a particular action.

Some critical and personal factors include the following:

- Values and beliefs
- Past experiences
- Current situation
- Personality

All these factors play roles in assessing someone's inner motivations, so it's essential to consider them all when trying to understand someone's buying behavior, i.e., their mood, readiness, and receptivity to your approach and message.

When considering their values and beliefs, ask yourself some of these following questions:

- What is important to them?
- What do they believe in?
- What do they stand for or stand against?

These factors play significant roles in what motivates someone. For example, someone who values helping others may be more motivated to volunteer for a charity than someone who doesn't share that value. Similarly, someone who believes that hard work will pay off may be more likely to persevere through a difficult task than someone who doesn't have that belief. Understanding the values and beliefs felt to be important to someone can give them a better understanding of what motivates them.

Similarly, keep in mind how a person's past experiences play a role in their motivation. For example, someone who has had a lot of success in the past may be more motivated to achieve more success. On the other hand, someone who has experienced failure may be more motivated to avoid failure. Past experiences shape our values and beliefs, and affect our current behavior. As appropriate, you always want to probe for a client's past experiences.

There are no definitive answers to the question of personality, and I would advise against trying to play amateur psychologist. It is, however, interesting to ponder the different personality types and how these might correspond to Maslow's hierarchy of needs.

For example, extroverted people may find their social needs more important than their needs for safety and self-actualization. This is not to say introverts do not have these needs as they may simply emphasize them less.

Conversely, highly analytical people may focus on their needs for intellectual stimulation and self-actualization more than their social or emotional needs. Again, this is not to say that other personality types do not have these same needs, but rather that they may emphasize them less.

Ultimately, understanding how different personality types relate to Maslow's hierarchy provides insights into why people with different personality types have different priorities. The more you sense, pick up, or get them to open up and tell you about their true priorities, the more you will feel the pulse of their hidden desires.

When it comes to their current situation, one thing you must do as a salesperson is size people up very quickly. I believe it is possible to be a "natural salesperson," and I believe I am one. I also believe professional sales skills can be taught, as I've had many years of sales training all of my life, and some of it has been indispensable. I believe deep within myself that sales mastery can be taught, which is why I've written this book.

What I am saying here is whether you are a natural at sizing up people or whether sizing up your clients is a learned skill, you must still assess the most effective way to communicate with the person in front of you at any particular moment. That is what I meant when I used the phrase, "sizing the person up."

However, it's crucial not to fall into the biases that can creep into your mind without warning. Unchallenged bias on your part can lull you to sleep and cause you to miss a signal that clues you into your client's unspoken desires. You may immediately come across many openly stated or seemingly apparent desires. Still, if you only go with what's on the surface, you'll miss an untold number of sales over time. Not only will you miss out on higher numbers of sales, but you'll also miss out on higher sales dollars and high client retention rates. You and your clients will miss out on much more than either of you deserve, or else, your clients will find what they deserve somewhere else, which is most likely to happen.

It sounds like we are taking a macro view of our client's buying behavior using Maslow's Hierarchy of Needs as a starting point and trying to extrapolate further data about their potential hopes and desires. I get that. But the intent is to zoom out as far as you can so that you can zoom back in as you move long the 7-step sales process. Any little clues you can pick up for yourself as to why your client wants to buy from you right now—reasons they aren't talking about yet or may never talk about—is something you can keep in your pocket for later.

You Must Know Them Better Than They Know Themselves

Salespeople must know their clients better than the clients know themselves to be successful. They must research their customers thoroughly and understand their needs, wants, and desires. Only then can they provide the products or services that genuinely meet their customers' needs. Salespeople who take the time to get to know their customers in great depth will be more successful in the long run.

There are a few key ways to gain insights into your customers. First, you need to perform thorough research on your target market. This includes understanding their demographics, psychographics, and buying behaviors. Once you have this information, you can begin to understand what motivates them and what drives their decision-making process.

Second, you need to establish a relationship with your customers. This can be done through regular communications via emails, phone calls, or face-to-face interactions. Get to know them personally and find out what their needs are. Only then will you be able to provide them with the solutions they're looking for.

Third, you need to constantly monitor your customers' behavior. Keep track of their buying patterns and how they interact with your product or service. This will give you valuable insight into their wants and needs. By understanding your customers better than they understand themselves, you'll be able to give them exactly what they want, and that's how you'll succeed in sales.

Throughout the following chapters, you and I will discuss how everything comes together into a beautiful blend culminating in your concrete mastery of the inner game of selling. As I said earlier, we're starting at the beginning of the sales conversation eyeball to eyeball with a client, most likely metaphorically.

In the Acknowledgments, I was not exaggerating when I said that I've been on the front lines of selling and in the driver's seat of an engine that drives the world's economy. Face-to-face selling, when you think of it, is the oldest profession in the world. I know plenty of folks say prostitution is the oldest profession in the world, but even prostitution comes down to making a sale, as a sale is almost always paid in advance.

Let me also reiterate that the principles here, which are as old as time and universal, are simply being conveyed through the lens of my life story. They are applicable to any form of sales, including business to business, which I've also done for years as a wholesaler and complex technical sales.

Okay, so I haven't personally sold high-technical goods yet—it's all the same. I've played an integral part in the many complex multi-stage sales transactions that required pitching a proposal to cross-functional teams across nationwide boundaries with multiple stakeholders and multiple decision-makers, and millions of dollars on the line.

But when you boil it all down, you come back to dealing with people and their wants, needs, and desires. At least, I'm sure I read that somewhere. My thesis is that the level of desire we must tap into is invisible to the naked eye until we take the time to look for that which cannot be seen from the surface.

You must know them better that they know themselves.

Ok, so now I'm a freshman in high school and still a kid. After my seasonal job at Winkelman's, I went to another place where my mom always shopped, the Sample House. The owners built a business by buying and reselling samples from large fashion houses, thus the name Sample House. One of the owners, Joe, read *Women's Wear Daily* (WWD). I would always ask Joe if I could have his copies of the magazine once he was done.

WWD is a fashion trade publication founded in 1910 by Edmund Fairchild and has been headquartered in New York City since its inception. WWD was known as the Fashion Bible and has been influential in fashion and business for over a century. Again, just a first-year student in high school, but I'm reading WWD from cover to cover twice whenever I have the chance. If there were anything from anybody of substance related to fashion, it would be in WWD.

One day Joe looked at me and asked, "Are you *really* reading *Women's Wear Daily*?" Not only was I reading it, but I could readily engage Joe or any of the owners with the latest trends, observations, and predictions in every aspect of fashion. And to put the icing on the cake, I could correlate what I was reading back to the impact it might have on the Sample House's buying patterns, advertising, promotional needs, and sales forecasts. Joe made sure I kept getting his copies of WWD.

Remember, we're just keeping my experience in the fashion world as a lens. True, I had a passion for the field, and that is not an absolute requirement for success, but it certainly does help a lot. The point is that I learned everything I could about the field I was engaged in from top to bottom and everything I could about the tastes, habits, goals, dreams, and desires of my clientele. Then I took that information and fused it together in a way that I could make practical use of it every day.

The front cover of WWD always had dazzling images of the latest fashion, and the headlines were always something noteworthy about a high-end designer doing something or other or else a fashion industry giant making a big splash. When you opened WWD, you would see loads of avant-garde fashions and designer sketches and get the latest scoop about anybody doing anything. Inside were also in-depth features on manufacturers, retailers, models, celebrities, trends, statistics, and of course, runway coverage. WWD was required study, and I was never late to class.

Another aspect of WWD that caught my rapt attention were the employment ads in the back. Ninety percent of the jobs were in New York. That's when I started dreaming about life in the Big Apple. I must admit I also had teenage dreams of becoming a fashion model. In the end, I went to New York and got a shot at modeling, but unfortunately, at 5 feet 6 inches, I was too short for the runway.

Now you may be asking how can all this New York City high-fashion industry hoo-hah could benefit a teenage salesgirl in Cleveland, Ohio? Well, I am glad you asked. All of that up-to-the-minute knowledge of the fashion world enabled me to tell my customers things they did not know and were not going to hear from anyone else.

I could say, "Hey, look, this is what everybody's going to be wearing next year. You can be one of the first ladies around town sporting this." "This just came out, straight from New York; it's sure to be the latest trend. I know you don't want to miss out." "These are the hottest colors for the coming year." "This designer is producing this, and this will be the new sensation, pretty soon it's going to be everywhere; you'll look great in this." "It's going to be short skirts this year; they are going to go up to here." "It's going to be long skirts this year. They'll be going down to there." It was the same thing with shoes, bags, and other accessories. It was all in *Women's Wear Daily.*

My clients loved it because I gave them reliable insights and information that they were not getting anywhere else. It was pivotal to my success as a young saleswoman that I could tell my clients what was hot and what was not. I was a teenage fashion maven who told them what was coming their way in the fashion world. And not only that, but I was helping them outfit themselves appropriately. The proof was having clients come back to me to tell me about all of the compliments they were getting from everyone who mattered (where is that on Maslow's Hierarchy?) and how spectacular they looked and felt after heeding my advice and wearing all of the things we had selected together.

This is where I came to understand how personal the world of selling is. You provide knowledge and insight that can help someone live a better life, and not only get paid for doing it but get paid handsomely. Well, I knew I had stumbled on to something big. I began to promote myself as a fashion coordinator.

As time moved on and I moved on to other stores, I eventually had to start buying my own subscription to *Women's Wear Daily*. I remember the yearly subscription being $19, which would be over $100 in 2022. Quite a sum for a teenager in the late-1970s to cough up, but it was well worth the investment for a young fashion coordinator.

Selling to Emotions

Salespeople used to be told to stick to the facts and avoid getting emotional. But the truth is today, and always has been, that emotion is a powerful tool in selling. And when it comes to closing a deal, logic and reason don't always prevail. Think about it: When you're making a purchase, whether it's a car or a pair of shoes, you're not just looking at the price tag. You're considering how the product makes you feel. Do you feel good about it? Do you feel like it's worth the money? In short, emotions play a significant role in the buying decision. That's why salespeople who can tap into their customer's emotions are more likely to consummate the deal.

The latest science tells us this is why emotions are more important in selling than logic and reason:

1. People make buying decisions based on emotions, not logic.
2. Emotions are more powerful than logic.
3. Emotions create loyalty and customer retention.
4. Emotionally driven marketing is more effective than rational marketing.
5. Emotional selling creates customers for life.

It helped me so much in my early career that I was immersed in an industry that was all about emotion. Let's face it, some of the far-out frocks you see on the runway and in the newspapers, tabloids, and fashion magazines are not functional attire. They are all about sensation and visceral impact. They are all about feelings and emotions. They are all about who the woman becomes when she wears a designer outfit and how other women will either love her, envy her, or hate her (or maybe all three and score the trifecta) because of what's on her body.

Sales is all about understanding and appealing to emotion. Prospects and customers make decisions based on their feelings, not logic or reason. The latest scientific data tell us that sometimes buying decisions are irrational. As salespeople, our job is to provide enough logic and reason for our clients to justify their emotional decision.

A few of the ways to tap into your clients' emotional needs include the following:

1. Study what motivates people to buy. What are the emotions that drive people to take action?

2. Study what prospects and customers in the industry care about. When you understand what matters to clients, you can appeal to those emotional needs throughout your sales conversation.

3. Be sure to get clarity in your own mind about your client's emotional needs and how what you have satisfied those needs. You must especially account for areas where your product or service falls short and how you can honestly and transparently account for and mitigate those areas of concern.

4. When talking to a client, pay attention to the words they use. Pay attention to what they say. What language do they use to describe their problem? What are their goals? Their answers will give you clues about their emotional needs.

5. Listen to their vocal tone. In addition to paying attention to the words your client uses, listen for clues in their tone of voice.

6. Use stories to connect with your audience. Stories are a powerful way to connect with people emotionally. When you tell a story about how your product or service has helped someone, it helps your client visualize how it could help them.

7. Appeal to their senses. In addition to using stories, you can also appeal to your client's senses in your sales presentation. Use language that evokes positive feelings, and make sure your visuals support your emotional message.

8. Paint a picture of how your product or service will make them feel after the sale (maybe even months or years after the sale if appropriate) and why that feeling is important to them now. You are selling them the future today.

9. Use emotions in your marketing materials. Use language that evokes positive feelings, and make sure your visuals support your emotional message. Your website, brochures, and other marketing materials should also appeal to emotions.

10. Practice using emotional selling techniques. The more you practice selling to emotions, the better you'll be at it. Try using emotional selling techniques in role-playing exercises with colleagues or practice in real sales situations, especially when you feel like there's nothing to lose.

Key Takeaways in Chapter 1

- Maslow's hierarchy of needs is only a starting point when attempting to assess human motivation for any reason and certainly when we are looking for a client's buried treasures—their hidden desires.
- The level of desire we must tap into is invisible to the naked eye until you take the time to look for that which cannot be seen from the surface.
- The latest science tells us this is why emotions are more important in selling than logic and reason.
- Sales is all about understanding and appealing to emotions. Prospects and customers make decisions based on their feelings, not logic or reason. The latest scientific data tells us that sometimes buying decisions are irrational.

As salespeople, our job is to provide enough logic and reason for our clients to justify their emotional decision.

Chapter 2

CONNECT WITH ANYONE, ANYWHERE, ANYTIME

*Each contact with a human being is so rare,
so precious, one should preserve it.*
Anais Nin

I must warn you. At this point, my story is going to start skipping around a little bit so bear with me. I'll catch you up to where we are right now. As I said in the Preface (if you read it; if you didn't, please go back now and take a peek—I'll wait). In the mid-1970s, I made today's equivalent of about $15,000 per year part-time in retail sales. I was given my first store management job at 17. I graduated from John Fitzgerald Kennedy High School Class of 1975 (a year early) and was accepted to Yale University.

While my mother loosened the apron strings enough to let me take my first sales job, she would sooner make Beelzebub grits and eggs for breakfast than allow her baby girl to spend four years out of her sight in New Haven, Connecticut. So I went to Cleveland State University instead—not at all a fair trade.

Eventually, as I knew it would, the overpowering allure of the New York City fashion scene claimed its next captive—me. Pressing the fast-forward button on my story for just a moment, I had an exciting, but very short-lived, modeling career because, at 5 foot 6 inches tall, I was too short for the runway. Nevertheless, modeling dreams notwithstanding, I was beginning to make a name for myself in the fashion and luxury sales community in the Big Apple.

One of my favorites and, in many ways, career-defining moments occurred when I worked for Villeroy & Boch, a world-renowned provider of high-quality ceramics, crystal, and tableware. The company was founded in 1748 in Mettlach, Germany. Villeroy & Boch has a reputation for innovation and excellence that is several centuries old. In 1766, Villeroy & Boch was the first to introduce printed decoration on ceramics. In 1789, it launched the world's first porcelain dinner service. Villeroy & Boch is still renowned for its beautiful and stylish tableware, sold in more than 130 countries worldwide. The company's products are used by some of the world's most prestigious hotels and restaurants, as well as discerning clients worldwide who appreciate the beauty and quality of their products. Oh, yes, I sold there for a little while.

Anyhow, I had just gotten started with Villeroy & Boch when I received an invite to attend a companywide sales meeting in Germany. I was a working mom with my first of three sons. I'll spare you the long story.

But the punchline is that I was unduly detained and missed my early morning plane to Germany from Newark—not at all a good look for a new employee. I was supremely panicked, as you can imagine. Now I had to leave Newark and race to JFK Airport, where the last flight to Germany I could get that day was going to take off. Mind you, I had four suitcases and a handbag while negotiating my way back from Newark to Queens. I was also dressed to the nines because I always have to look good no matter where I go, even on an eight-hour, nonstop, international flight to Frankfurt. But you can bet I was wearing sensible shoes.

I was sure my other Villeroy & Boch colleagues were all on the earlier flight, and so I was on my own. I took three years of German in high school, and I was a straight-A student, of course. I loved the language and thought my high school German would help me get by. Well, not so much after I landed in Frankfurt the next morning, when I'm sure I looked like the typical dazed and confused American tourist.

Anyway, I'm in this airport, wandering around asking questions, or at least I thought I was. From the puzzling looks, vague shrugs, and aimless pointing, I felt like I might well be trying to communicate with the Duchess, the Cheshire Cat, and the March Hare. Even though I was the only one who had fallen down a rabbit hole. Darn, that White Rabbit. I, too, was late for a very important date.

I made it outside of that maze of an airport, and I found a taxi. My plan was to take this taxi from Frankfurt to Mettlach, which I thought was only a couple of hours away, but it turned out to be a bit longer. I took Klaus, the first driver who smiled and waved and immediately went for my bags. I managed to negotiate with him where I needed to go with all the high school German I could command. He understood Villeroy & Boch and where I needed to go. That was good enough for me, and we took off.

Klaus was a stout and powerfully built, gray-and-silver-haired gentleman. His movements were swift and his manner deliberately business-like, but he seemed to smile very easily. I was a young, thin, attractive woman in a country I'd never set foot in before and going from one town to another all by myself. I was pitching myself into the complete unknown and putting my life in the hands of a stranger. All I knew was that I had something to do, and I had to get it done.

There was a half-smoked pipe in the front ashtray of his car, and though I am not a fan of smoking anyway, the inside of his taxi had the faint smell of an earthy cologne. As we traveled down the road with the windows open, the morning air around us was light and vibrant, with immaculate blue skies above. Rolling down the road, I gazed tranquilly at the trees, hedges, and fields rushing by in their orderly and elegant shades of green. We got halfway through this incredibly beautiful landscape dotted with curiosity-inspiring little towns, and suddenly, the car started coughing and sputtering.

Klaus pulled off to the side of the road. He was talking to me in German. I didn't understand a bit of it, but what I did understand didn't sound good. I felt like he was saying, "This is when I kill you." I mean, I jumped on a plane to a foreign country, and I had no idea where I really was. *What do I do?* I'm thinking like, *this guy is probably going to kill me.*

Klaus got out of the car and walked all around. I searched as far as I could see up and down the road. Nothing on the horizon in either direction. What wouldn't I give for a good old-fashion Fifth Avenue traffic jam right now.

Klaus looked under the hood, said a few more things in German that sounded like *Get ready to say your prayers now*, and he got back into the car and continued driving. *Oh, great, I'm thinking. He's taking me somewhere else to kill me. This is just great.*

I felt relieved for the moment once Klaus picked up the radio handset in his taxi and called into dispatch. There was a woman on the other end of the line who seemed to be giving him directions. *This is good,* I thought. I was hoping there might be a nearby taxi station where we could get a replacement vehicle or even a garage that might make a quick repair.

Where we ended up wasn't a taxi station or a garage. It seemed to be someone's home. The door opened, and a stately, older woman with hair darker than her age stepped out of the house. She was taller than Klaus and looked like she was quite a beauty in her day. She looked at him and then she looked at me with equal inquisitiveness.

A huge St. Bernard came bursting out of the door. The dog stopped and looked at me. Then that massive pooch ran up to Klaus, wanting and waiting to be petted. At that moment, I knew this must be Klaus's home.

Klaus introduced me to Karla. My next sigh of relief came when Karla spoke some broken English in my general direction. Between the two of them, they let me know another taxi was coming. In the meantime, I was welcome to come in and wait.

Klaus and Karla had a simple home, spacious and plain, bare but solid. Karla made coffee and warmed up rolls left over from breakfast. Though we didn't say much, we shared the placid glances of strangers patiently biding time. Everything seemed comfortable enough, except for me being allergic to Otto the dog.

After about an hour, another taxi finally arrived. As I bid goodbye to Klaus and Karla to resume my adventure to Mettlach, Klaus asked me to pay him the full fare, even though, by his own estimation, we were only halfway there. Suddenly, my German got much better. Come to think of it, my German rose up to a college-graduate level in about 10 seconds. I started rattling all of it off like a native speaker. Here is the English version of my tirade.

"First of all, we've only gotten halfway. Second of all, your car broke down, not only causing me extreme inconvenience but also putting me in potential danger, and then I have to pay this second taxi driver for the rest of the trip—you're totally out of your mind, brother."

I coughed up exactly half the fare and counted it out flawlessly in German marks. Then grabbing and holding the bottom of his hand, I looked Klaus dead in the eyes and slammed the money into the palm of his hand.

He looked at me and then he looked at Karla, a wide-eyed stunned expression frozen on his face. Karla looked at him, and then she looked at me and burst out laughing. Klaus knew it was game over. He turned on his heels and walked away. I thanked Karla and said a grateful goodbye, while Klaus and the new driver loaded my luggage into the new taxi.

The second driver never said anything. I never got his name. He was a much younger man, a blue-eyed blonde. He nodded a lot, but barely uttered a word though I was speaking what I felt was fairly simple but pretty decent German. He let his nodding do the talking. I did catch him taking glances at me in the rearview mirror. All the same, he never uttered so much as "Gesundheit" when I sneezed. I imagined he was thinking, *I best not say anything to this crazy American woman. She might kill me.*

The rest of the ride was just as idyllic as the first part, even in the unbroken silence. Ninety minutes later, I stepped out of the taxi, as I'd reached the Villeroy & Boch headquarters by lunchtime.

I paid the remaining part of the fare but didn't have cash left for a tip. I ran inside the building, found out where the company luncheon was being held, ran in there like a crazy American woman, and started asking who might be able to float me two bucks.

People came up to me, simultaneously welcoming me and asking me what was going on.

"What do you mean?"

"Why do you need two dollars?"

"Who are you, by the way?"

I told them all who I was: a new employee from the New York store who was here for the company meeting, and I ran out of cash and I needed two more dollars because I had a taxi outside and I needed to tip the taxi driver.

It took a while to actually get the tip, and I'm surprised the guy waited. But I'm glad that he did because my bags were still outside. For what seemed like hours, but could only have been a few minutes, several more people walked up to find out what was going on. The rest of the people remained at their lunch tables, shifting in their chairs, venturing glances, and sometimes craning their necks to look around other people's heads.

One of the managers I had met in New York during the hiring process apparently walked outside, came back in, and said to everyone, "Ach so, there is a taxi out there."

One figure cut through the flash mob I'd created by this time: Bernard, the company president. I went through my frenzied retelling one more time for Bernard. He took me in from head to toe for a moment, then burst out laughing.

I did not know that I was the first one from the second group from the States to get there. Everyone else had been stuck at the airport and were just now boarding a train from Frankfurt to Mettlach.

Steven, one of the execs who had interviewed me in the States, gave me the money to run back out and give this poor guy a tip. Then I went back inside and had lunch. Obviously, I'd made quite an impression.

The rest of the team did not arrive until after dinnertime. They were all surprised to find out I'd been there since lunch. Some were at the airport while I was running around, distraught and bewildered. If I had run into any of them, I would have probably missed out on my taxi adventure and on making a big impression on Bernard.

Bernard was a lovely man, and throughout my time at Villeroy & Boch, he checked in on me. If he was in our store in New York, he never failed to come by and say, "Hi. How are you doing?" and sometimes, "Are you sure you don't need fare for a cab?"

Bernard used me as an example for the next couple of days, saying, "If Ruth could get to Germany all by herself and take a taxi to Mettlach, completely on her own, you can certainly do [so and so]."

All in all, this could have turned out much differently, but it turned into one of the most memorable and enjoyable of all my sales journeys so far. I met interesting people. I made unforgettable connections. I impressed the president of a storied international firm. I grew up about 10 years in one little trip. The truth is, I was young enough to be fearless, but I learned how to do what needed to be done.

Connectagility

This book is so short because I'm trying to get right to the point as quickly and simply as possible. If you haven't jumped to the back of the book already, which I do sometimes, I admit. Sometimes, I even start at the back and work my way forward because I'm always so anxious to get to the point.

Another reason why the book is so short is there's nothing new under the sun, so I don't want to belabor ideas you've already seen and heard. Instead, I am coaxing you to take what you already know and drive it down more deeply into your heart, soul, and whole way of being in the moment when you are dealing with someone you are selling.

Yet another reason this book is so short is that I am not teaching techniques. If you want sales techniques, there are libraries full of books and articles you can find all about sales techniques. And, of course, there's always Amazon. Then come back and reread this one again. Come to think of it, reread this one again anyway and tell all of your friends about it, too.

Have you ever met someone and instantly felt a connection? Maybe it was the way they looked at you or the way they made you laugh. Or maybe it was just a feeling that you couldn't explain. But what if there was a way to instantly form a personal connection with anyone, anywhere, anytime? It may sound impossible, but it's pretty simple. All you need to do is ask questions and care about the answers they give you.

By asking questions, you are showing interest in the other person. You are allowing them to share their thoughts and feelings with you. And when they do, you can connect with them on a deeper level. By caring about the answer, you send verbal and non-verbal messages that they are important. They matter.

You can instantly form a personal connection with anyone, anywhere, anytime by following these three simple steps:

Step 1. When you meet someone for the first time, look them in the eye and give them a genuine smile. It has to be genuine. Fake smiles are verboten. For the time you are with someone, focus the entirety of your being on them. This will help create an instant rapport. When you care about them and what they care about, you already have something in common.

Step 2. Reach common ground as quickly and often as possible. It could be anything as long as it is genuine, mutually shared loves or interests of any kind. Always search for clues in their manner, speech, clothing, general appearance, and surroundings. People love talking about themselves, so ask the other person questions about their life, their interests, and their opinions. Not only will this help you get to know them better, but it will also make them feel appreciated and valued.

The most important commonality you must establish and reinforce in their minds is that you both have their best interest in mind. You can't come out and say it. Every con artist says that. They have to see that you really do mean it. That's not a matter of technique. All of that comes from inside of you.

Step 3 is, when all else fails, remember Step 1. Remember that connection is not only fundamental to sales; it is fundamental to life.

When it comes to the 7-step sales process, remember we're still only in Step 2. We still have five more steps to go; people buy from people they like and trust, but that's not enough. I've liked and trusted lots of salespeople and didn't buy a darn thing. On the other hand, I never bought anything if I didn't like the salesperson. I would leave and come back if I had to (maybe).

Yet selling is not just liking and trusting. The client has to know or at least feel, *feel* being the operative word, that you share their goal to get the very best out of this transaction for them. They are totally okay with you getting a benefit, too, as long as the majority of that benefit comes from you helping them. I'm serious.

I heard the comedian Paul Mooney once say when an interviewer asked him how he was doing, "I'm just making phone calls from the Planet 'Me' like everybody else." We are all on the Planet "Me." If you are genuinely doing something to help Planet "Me," I am all about helping you do that. And so is everybody else.

Okay. I hear some of you saying, "Enough, enough, enough. So, how do you do that?" Well, some of you are not going to like the answer, but I'm giving it to you right between the eyes. You must place your needs, wants, and desires slightly out of focus for a brief time. Better yet, it would be best to pour their thoughts, needs, and desires straight into yours, thoroughly blending them like cream (or half-and-half) into your tea or coffee.

You have to try for whatever time it takes, and as quickly as possible, to not only understand but fully take on the entire perspective of the situation at hand and the future stage the customer is expecting to achieve from dealing with you, your company, and your product or service. Admittedly, this gets tricky when presenting to multiple people and personalities with competing needs and agendas. But stay with me for a moment because, in the end, sales are won or lost at personal and emotional levels.

Allow yourself to intensely step into the experience, thoughts, feelings, and perspectives of another human being without judgment or bias as quickly as you can for as long as the sales transaction lasts. Do it because you want to embody that experience as if it were your own, not for the sake of practicing a technique for but the sake of expanding yourself as a human being. Remember, you must work on the inner world first, and the outer world follows along later. When you're doing that, no matter what happens at the end of a sales conversation, you walk out of that engagement a better person. What's not to like about that?

My life has been exciting and fascinating, meeting, serving, and managing different people from different cultures world-wide. My interactions, both professionally and personal, have spanned a kaleidoscope of cultures. I admit that it can be a chal-lenge explaining things very well to people from another culture. This is especially true if you don't understand what is expected in their culture and how they communicate things based on the norms of their society. I don't claim to be a cultural expert. There are other books for that. Yet, when you can look someone in the face—not necessarily in the eyes—and make them know that for this frozen microsecond of time all you really want is what they also really want. As John Lennon said, "It's easy, if you try."

Also, keep in mind that our society has sub-cultures within its culture. As our population ages and lifespans expand, we often deal with five different generations:

1. Silent Generation, ages 80 years and older
2. Baby Boomers, ages 58 to 79
3. Generation X, ages 57 to 46
4. Millennials, ages 26 to 45
5. Generation Z, ages 25 to 7

For those old enough to recall, in 1977, Pepsi came out with the slogan, "Generation Next," after pinning Baby Boomers as the "Pepsi Generation" way back in 1963. This is only one exam-ple of how global brands, at one level, attempt to connect with the largest swath of their target audience. Today, micro-targeting and the concept of winning micro-moments in the customer's journey are rapidly gaining in urgency, utilization, and adoption.

All of this brings us back to connecting across cultures, sub-cultures, and multiple generations in the blink of an eye. Performing an operation that complex and seemingly insurmountable with grace and ease has to come from the willingness to embrace the things that are most common and fundamental to us all. I am calling it the *practical*, I repeat *practical*, application of the best of the human spirit has to offer. When you've got that, you've got something I call *connectagility*.

We Don't Buy Things, We Buy Feelings

When we go out to purchase something, we're not really buying the item alone. We're buying the feeling we hope to experience by owning that item. Whether it's a new car, a flashy piece of jewelry, or a designer handbag, as people, we want to feel happy, successful, and stylish. As people, that is part of the dream we all have for our lives. As sales professionals, we must focus on selling the feeling, not the product.

As sales professionals, we must focus on selling the feeling, not the product.

All of the science on the subject of selling, especially neuroscience, tells us that everyone sells best using stories. Back in the day, a salesperson was known as someone with a story to tell and something to sell. Therefore, it is no surprise that the latest and greatest information about how to sell includes the need to tell stories, the most important one being the story of your client's transformation as a result of buying your product or service.

You want to tell a story that speaks to the emotions your product evokes in your client, and you'll be more likely to move the needle towards your sale. For example, if you're selling a luxurious item, show your customer how it will make them feel rich and glamorous. Or, if you're selling a health supplement, highlight how it will give them more energy and help them lead a healthier life. Keeping in mind if you're selling multiple items to the same client, you may need to tap into multiple emotional touch points. Still, the more you tap into the dream, as we will talk about later, the more powerful and expansive your palette of vibrant, emotional colors to work with will be.

You see, it is all about demonstrating to the client on an emotional level how your product or service will make their life better or the life of someone they care about, which once again makes their life better.

It's all about how your product or service will make their life better or the life of someone they love better.

Always Be Connecting

I have two ABCs for you: always be connecting and always be celebrating.

The rules of always be connecting are as follows:

1. *Be genuine in your interactions with customers.* They can tell if you're being phony or disingenuous, and it will turn them off.
2. *Show interest in your customer as a person, not just as a potential sale.* Ask about their interests, their family,

and their day-to-day lives. Let them know that you care about them as human beings, not just as a means to an end.

3. *Always be professional, even if the customer is not.* It's essential to maintain your composure and keep your cool, no matter how challenging the situation.

This isn't namby-pamby, pseudo-science, woo-woo magic, new age tripe. You readily accept the idea of relating to your client. You accept the idea that people more readily like and accept people they feel are just like them. I'm only asking you to take what you believe to be accurate and ratchet it down a few more notches within your belief system. It's not that hard if you give it a try. Money isn't a side-hustle. It is a side-effect.

Success at anything isn't as much about what you do as it is about who you are. You can apply these concepts and the rest of the concepts in this book to your life. If that gets to be too much, then just shrink it down to the person you have to be when you are in a sales situation at any given time. But be careful. The thoughts and ideas in this book may spill over to your personal life if you're not paying attention. You might find yourself constantly looking for new ways to celebrate life. Bummer.

Money isn't a side-hustle. It's a side-effect.

Key Takeaways in Chapter 2

- To tune into your client, you must be willing to place your needs, wants, and desires slightly out of focus for a brief time. Better yet, blend their thoughts, needs, and desires straight into yours.
- To instantly build a connection with anyone, anywhere, anytime, all you need to do is ask questions and care about the answers they give you.
- By caring about the answers, you send verbal and non-verbal messages that they are important. By genuinely being interested in what the other person is interested in, you already have something important to them in common.
- We don't buy things. We buy feelings.
- Money isn't a side-hustle. It is a side-effect.
- Practical application of the best of what the human spirit can offer by being able to connect with grace and ease with multiple cultures and sub-cultures around the world and multiple sub-cultures within your own culture spanning five generations is *connectagility.*
- ABC = a̲lways b̲e c̲onnecting.

Always Be Connecting.

SOLVE THE PUZZLE

Chapter 3

EXPLORING THE UNDISCOVERED

Exploration is really the essence of the human spirit.
Frank Borman

continued making a name for myself in the retail sales industry in New York. I had recruiters calling quite often to pitch new opportunities, but I've always been very loyal. I never chased after the next hot job or the next explosive opportunity if I was happy and being treated well.

Speaking of recruiting, as a sales manager, I was afforded opportunities to recruit. I traveled all over the country interviewing and recruiting top sales talent. Like many women and men, I am sure, I admire Oprah Winfrey. The first time I saw Oprah on TV was during a recruiting engagement I had in Chicago. This was long before Oprah became the giant that she is today. The great part of watching Oprah for the first time and every time was that it was so easy to tell that she had it. Whatever it was, you knew for sure that this lady had it. I kind of felt like I had discovered something, which was ridiculous, of course, because she was already on TV.

I was in a very comfortable spot in my life when a recruiter called and described a potential opportunity to work for Nina Ricci, a fashion house founded by Maria "Nina" Ricci and her son Robert in 1932. The Nina Ricci brand became known for its romanticism and femininity, as exemplified by designs such as the apple-shaped perfume bottle created by Marc Lalique. In 1946, Nina Ricci designed the famous "Coque d'Or" dress worn by Audrey Hepburn in the film *Roman Holiday*. This helped solidify the brand's reputation as a go-to for red-carpet glamour.

Today, Nina Ricci is helmed by creative director Guillaume Henry, who has been with the brand since 2015. Under his direction, the house has continued to produce world-captivating designs that capture the essence of Nina Ricci.

I knew the name at the time mainly because of Nina Ricci's perfume. I didn't know what I was getting into, but I knew this was a high-end designer name, so I knew it obviously had to be an ample opportunity. I went for a first interview, which went well enough to have a second one. I also did well in the second interview, and they called me back for a third one. In the third interview, I met the company's two owners at that time. They interviewed me at the Harvard Club in Midtown Manhattan. I didn't understand at the time why I was being interviewed at the Harvard Club. I still felt my allegiance was with Yale anyway. No, seriously. I was only 26 and still very young in my career.

In hindsight, I understand I was being interviewed at the Harvard Club because one of them had graduated from Harvard and they wanted to see how I performed in an upscale social setting. I was schooled in the social graces at a very early age, thanks again to mom.

It all worked out well and I got the job: national sales manager for the Nina Ricci line of costume jewelry. It was an auspicious career move landing a national sales manager position with an 18-karat-gold company that manufactured 18-karat-gold jewelry, among many other things.

Nina Ricci's clothing line included everything from basics to eveningwear and all the accessories featuring a wide range of handbags, jewelry, and shoes.

The brand's fragrances were also very popular, and they offered a variety of scents to suit every woman's taste. At that time, I owned a bottle of L'air Du Temps perfume. It is in a beautiful Lalique crystal bottle with a bird in flight on the top. With top notes of carnation, aldehydes, rose, neroli, Brazilian rosewood, peach, and bergamot, and base notes of iris, oakmoss, musk, sandalwood, benzoin, amber, vetiver, and cedar. L'air Du Temps is a classic feminine musk—but I digress.

In addition to managing sales for the complete line of Nina Ricci costume jewelry, there was another line of business I found extremely exciting. Catherine Deneuve, the iconic French actress, had a line of jewelry being sold under a licensing agreement. Her jewelry line was soft, sophisticated, and radiantly elegant. I was responsible for building and increasing Nina Ricci's costume jewelry line market share throughout the United States. Oh, I almost forgot, they also owned the license for the Tag Heuer watch line, the ultimate reference in luxury chronograph watches. So, I felt I was traveling in good company.

My product lines were primarily manufactured in Toronto by Bijoux D'Orlan Jewelers. who manufactured for Nina Ricci in the U.S. and worldwide. I flew to Canada several times a year to buy the products I could sell to the U.S. jewelry market. I usually traveled with one of the owners, who listened to, and respected, my opinions on what would have the most appeal and the great potential to sell in the current market environment.

Remember me reading *Women's Wear Daily* cover to cover several times a day? I'm leaving out details of the hours I spent every evening gaining product knowledge, doing market research, analyzing competitors, and reading trade journals. I knew my stuff. I couldn't have gotten the job unless I had convinced both owners of that.

The results were phenomenal. Everything we selected each season was new, exciting, glamorous, and thought-provoking. The owners were savvy at managing exchange rates to ensure the best transfer pricing. My product lines were always a big hit and sold into every major department store, specialty stores, and fine jewelers. Industry experts highly reviewed the products we selected as being intricate and beautifully designed enough that you could introduce them right alongside the finest authentic jewelry.

At that time, I had quite the career on my hands. I also had another thing on my hands, or more accurately, in my abdomen. I had a second son coming on board. Please understand that I know I am not the only woman in the world to sacrifice her career for the sake of her family, far from it. In fact, I know many of us make that choice multiple times in a lifetime. The same goes for me. I made a choice for family over career more times than I recall. But if I had to do it again, I would still choose to be a mother over making a career move if push came to bulldozer.

To have the opportunities I had at such a young age, relatively speaking, is something I will always cherish, just as much as I cherish my family. But have no fear as my career saga did continue.

Now might be the time to bring up that the See-Solve-Satisfy (S^3) method has a companion parallel process with three phases. I haven't coined a name like S^3 for these: high intention, high clarity, and high resonance. What a minute. I changed my mind. Let's call them High^3. I like the sound of that, don't you? S^3 and High^3.

High intention, high resonance, high clarity (High^3)
the S^3 method leverages High^3 throughout the process.

In the previous two chapters, we talked about high intention, which is the intention to perform a Vulcan mind meld with the client, where we see, touch, taste, smell, think, and perceive everything precisely as our client would in this circumstance.

If you can accept the idea of trying to get on the same page with a client, trying to speak the client's language, making sure you're trying to sell the client the way the client likes to buy, and selling the client using stories and imagery, then you're already in tune with the idea of H^3.

Our goal in achieving sales mastery is to drive this intention down to the deepest level of appreciation, understanding, and behavior so that we can transform our way for the sake of our clients' best interests. As we are gear-shifting from seeing to solving and ultimately satisfying, we are not moving from H^3. Instead, we are infusing H^3 throughout the solve process, which

I am comparing to a puzzle, and there are multiple puzzles to be solved, so it is more like a 3D puzzle. Yet the two major variables you will have to solve for are the sales strategy (specific approach for this client) and the sales solution (how you will deliver your client to the Promised Land).

I've got one friend who always says people are always trying to overcomplicate things. All we really need to do is ask the right questions. It's hard to argue with that as so much of that is true. The only trick is figuring out what are the right questions.

In the exploration phase, we use questions like shovels and backhoes to help us get below the surface of our client's stated needs. Similarly, during the discovery phase, we want to thoroughly examine everything unearthed with kid gloves in our explorations while continuing to explore those areas yet to come (so far as they are relevant to achieving the desired outcome). Selling is about messaging, but you won't have a message that will trigger the client's desire to buy until you've gathered enough information to put all the pieces of the strategy and sales solution puzzle together.

The Key to Skillful Questioning

Going back now to this question: Which questions should you ask? Each of the 7 components—desire, connection, exploration, discovery, selection, consummation, and celebration—are meant to build upon one another.

The information you gather is from your thorough analysis of their stated and hidden desires and the things you come to better understand about the client as you build and deepen your business and interpersonal connections. This information lays the groundwork for the appropriate questions you must start targeting to solve the puzzle of what solutions you are offering best serve your client's needs at this particular time. You also want to know the best ways to structure a solution that you can go along with to help your clients make a selection, consummate the arrangement, and then celebrate the outcome you co-created that will bring enormous benefit to your client, possibly for years to come.

The Socratic selling method is a unique sales approach that uses questions to lead customers to their own conclusions. This technique can be used in various situations, including when a client is unsure about a product or service, when they need more information, or when they want to be sure they are making the right decision. This type of selling is beneficial because it allows you to maintain control of the conversation while still allowing the client to feel like they are in control.

The Socratic selling method is named after the Greek philosopher Socrates, known for using questioning to elicit answers from others. The Socratic selling method is based on the belief that people have all the answers within them but sometimes need help finding those answers. In the context of sales, you must skillfully use questions to guide the clients to the correct conclusions. The three key features of the Socratic selling method are:

1. **Listening actively:** This means listening carefully and asking questions to help clarify stated needs and uncover hidden ones.
2. **Helping the customer find their own answers:** Our goal must be to help the client find their own answers,

rather than telling them what to do. This means avoiding giving unsolicited advice or suggestions.

3. **Encouraging decision-making:** We should encourage clients to make their own decisions and offer them support along the way. This includes helping the client weigh various options and providing resources to help them make an informed decision.

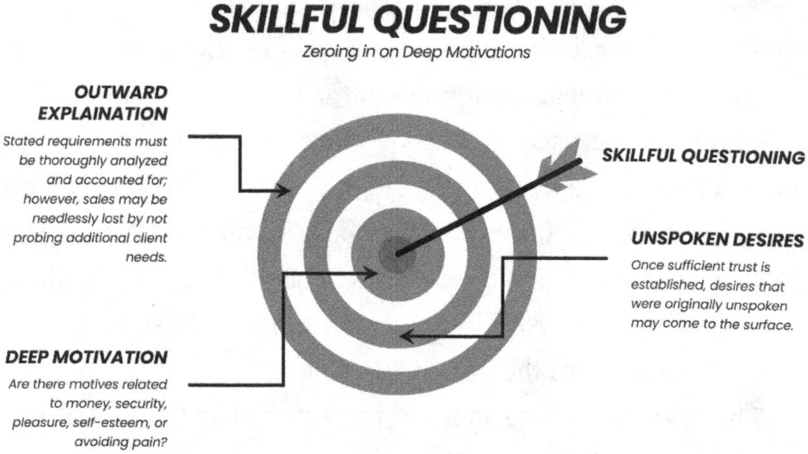

SKILLFUL QUESTIONING
Zeroing in on Deep Motivations

OUTWARD EXPLAINATION

Stated requirements must be thoroughly analyzed and accounted for; however, sales may be needlessly lost by not probing additional client needs.

SKILLFUL QUESTIONING

UNSPOKEN DESIRES

Once sufficient trust is established, desires that were originally unspoken may come to the surface.

DEEP MOTIVATION

Are there motives related to money, security, pleasure, self-esteem, or avoiding pain?

Figure 4. Skillful Questioning Targets Unrevealed Motivation

Agile Selling

There is a concept in technology and particularly in software development called Agile.

Agile software development is, at its heart, a set of software development practices based on the Manifesto for Agile Software Development, first published in 2001. The Agile Manifesto outlines 12 key principles that agile developers adhere to today in order to deliver high-quality software products.

The main idea is that instead of delivering one complete solution that may or may or may not meet the client's needs for a variety of reasons (e.g., miscommunication of requirements, needs to be changed in mid-process, technical flaws discovered too late, etc.) the agile process delivers smaller chunks of the soon-to-be-delivered product that the client can review and examine before the entire process is packaged together and delivered. It's kind of like cooking a large meal but taste testing everything along the way.

You are constantly checking in with the client and getting feedback that the puzzle pieces fit correctly. When you find out there is a piece of your soon-to-be-proposed solution that doesn't fit, you can search for the correct piece to put in its place. In the software world, that's called iterative and incremental development. In the selling world, we call it staying attuned or tuned in to your client. In the 1970s, we called it getting "micro-commitments" along the way.

Let me point out this requires mindfulness and transparency. It also requires tailoring and re-tailoring your sales strategy based on incoming information as it lands, so that we stay true to our product, service, and company. We remain nimble in our approach, but firm on our principles to serve the client's best interests.

Suppose that at any time incoming information makes it clear that the best course of action for the client is a recommendation, which I will refer to as a "no sale." If a "no sale" outcome is genuinely the best outcome for the client, then the celebration of that "no sale" is just as legitimate as the celebration of a sale (though not nearly as large and enthusiastic in most cases).

Let me take a moment to say this once again: If you and your client have honestly determined that there is a better or a different solution from the solution you have to offer at this time, then a "no sale" conclusion is cause for celebration. The exploration phase is typically too early to make that final determination without more data, but sometimes a client can disqualify themselves shortly after saying, "Hello."

We owe it to ourselves and our client to thoroughly examine the logic, reasoning, and emotions along the path of a "no sale"—but we should never be afraid of a "no" or a "no sale" if it truly benefits the client's best interest. We should never be afraid of the word *no* or of engaging in a conversation that may lead down a path ending in "no sale."

A "no sale" may just mean you've done your job, and you've done it well. But you couldn't haven't done it well if you've missed an opportunity to discover hidden benefits, correct potential misperceptions, and clarify ideas and concepts that might help your client make a better decision. This is why we engage in skillful exploration and must continue to adapt our sales strategy to the client on an ongoing basis.

Zero in on Their Pain

Your client's pain is the driving force behind the whole sales process. Without understanding and addressing their pain, you will severely limit your ability to help them see for themselves why your solutions are in their best interest. By taking the time to discover their specific pain points, you can develop a tailored solution that truly meets their needs. Only by solving your client's pain can you hope to reach that lofty goal we are calling satisfaction.

Only by solving your client's pain can you hope to reach that lofty goal we are calling satisfaction.

Targeting your client's pain can be done in several ways. One of the most effective ways is to simply ask questions that help you understand their situation and look for areas where you can see struggle, discomfort, and frustration or an area that the client appears to actively avoid talking about—if you can get there tactfully.

Be both direct and empathetic. You want to make sure that you are getting to the root of the problem so that you can offer a solution, but you also don't want to come across as pushy or insensitive. If an area seems sensitive for any reason, leave it alone until you have more clarity from the client about the nature of the area.

One way to strike a balance is to ask more questions about their current situation and what other problems they are trying to solve. If they seem hesitant to share, let them know that you're only trying to understand what they're dealing with so that you can see if there's anything you can do to help.

Once they open up, really listen to what they're saying. Ask follow-up questions to get more information and look for patterns. What are the main pain points that keep coming up? What seems to be causing the most frustration?

With this new information in hand, you can start to craft a solution that will address your client's specific needs. Target their pain, but then give them complete freedom and release of that pain through your solution(s) later in the process. You will find that because you took the time to really understand their pain points, they'll be more likely to trust that you have their best interests at heart.

Key Takeaways in Chapter 3

- Our goal must be to help the client find their own answers, rather than telling them what to do. We should encourage clients to make their own decisions and offer them support along the way. This includes helping the client weigh various options and providing resources to help them make an informed decision.

- Finding that a client is not an appropriate candidate for a sale at this time is still a just cause for celebration. Typically, however, the exploration phase is too early to make that kind of discovery.

- Your client's pain is the driving force behind the sales process. Without understanding and addressing their pain, you will severely limit your ability to help them see for themselves why your solutions are in their best interest.

Chapter 4

DISCOVERY AND DENOUEMENT

The more original a discovery,
the more obvious it seems afterward.
Arthur Koestler

If you remember your Sherlock Holmes, not the CBS television series Elementary with Jonny Lee Miller or the BBC television series Sherlock with Benedict Cumberbatch (both of which I am a huge fan), but the original detective novels written by Sir Arthur Conan Doyle, you remember that Holmes had a very specific method. Holmes took in all of the information that was available about the case from various sources, be it the client themselves, participants or subjects in the case, Inspector Lestrade from Scotland Yard, and occasionally the Baker Street Irregulars, a squad of street-smart juveniles that cold cull together intelligence from all over London.

Holmes gathered all the facts and information first and analyzed various bits and pieces along the way to determine which pieces were relevant to the puzzle. Then and only then, using the process of deductive reason, he did whatever it took to fit all the pieces into the perfect puzzle. Once the puzzle was completed, he presented it while revealing the crime, the motive, the criminal, and the absolute proof of all three. The process we have come to recognize in detective fiction from Adrian Monk to Aurelio Zen is the denouement.

Similarly, during the S^3 method, we pull all of the pieces together to solve a puzzle, otherwise known as our sales strategy and solution. Once we have gathered all the facts and analyzed which facts are relevant, including uncovering all the salient facts that may have been buried under the surface or otherwise hidden from view, our next move is to discover how everything fits together. This is a process we go through with the client, not something we do to the client.

A Winning Sales Strategy + a Winning Sales Solution = Puzzle Solved.

This is the new paradigm in modern sales, where all of the power has shifted to the side of the client and not the seller anymore. People will no longer tolerate having things done to them, but people always enjoy having things done for them and with them. That is not to say that clients cannot or should not ever be guided. The client's solutions should be discovered with the client involved. In an ideal collaboration, leading and following should flow back and forth, I won't say easily, but it should be a readily available option at any time in the process.

I've been in luxury brands for most of my sales career, selling to the wealthy and affluent, especially in the state of New York and most of the time in Manhattan. I spent a little over a decade working at Villeroy & Boch. I had so many wonderful experiences at that company outside of my three trips to Germany, each one being better than the one before. I was district manager over five luxury stores that generated $6.1 million annually, leading operations, recruiting, training, and mentoring 40–50 member sales teams that delivered outstanding sales and customer service. During my tenure, I also facilitated the opening of five new stores and achieved multiple honors and recognitions, including the 1999 and 2000 "Highest Achievement in People Development Award" and nomination in 2006 and 2007 for the "Manager of The Year & Best Sales Performance Award."

Out of all the many things I treasure most about my experiences at Villeroy & Boch was the opportunity to be mentored and coached by Isabelle Von Boch. Isabelle is an eighth-generation family member of a now 274-year-old company. If you were to have dinner with the Pope or many of the Royal Families left around the world, which according to Google, there are still 26, you would probably be eating your words, I mean, exchanging bon mots surrounded by Villeroy & Boch dinnerware.

Isabelle grew very fond of me, and I am especially fond of her. Isabelle is, to this day, one of my most cherished mentors, of which I do have a few. Having mentors along the way is important if you can find them. I know, I know, this just in, breaking news: find yourself a mentor. I started with Mrs. Russell, who hired me for my first sales position. I'm sure when I walked in that first day, she saw the shoes I was wearing and knew that I wouldn't last in those shoes for half of my shift. Even as I hid behind the counter in my bare feet, she never said a word. She only walked by occasionally and asked how I was doing, but she always looked out for me like a mother, and I'll never forget her.

The first time I met Isabelle, I was scheduled for a sales manager's training. Only three managers were selected for this training, and it was one-on-one or three-on-one with Isabelle. Even during the first training session, Isabelle took to me immediately. I became one of the managers who picked her up from the airport, drove her to various events, or drove her to her stores to visit. Isabelle was always so excited to visit her stores, and everyone was always excited to see her. She had an infectious smile. She was so magnetic, with incredible grace and generosity.

Isabelle would often say, "You know, you can eat your food off paper plates every day; if that's what you want to do, that's fine. But I'm telling you, everything tastes better on fine dinnerware." I remember when I would slip up and say, "China," I would hear, "China is a place. This is dinnerware." However, I've noticed that in Villeroy & Boch's videos and blog posts lately, they will refer to fine dinnerware as China. Times do change, and we must also change with them.

Discovery Is Detective Work

A professional salesperson is like a detective because we are always looking for clues and trying to uncover new information. We are constantly asking questions to get to the bottom of whatever we are selling. In addition, as salespeople, we are always looking for ways to uncover clients' needs and resolve them. Finally, as sales detectives, we must never give up on the case and never give up on doing all that it takes to improve our craft.

- Both salespeople and detectives need to be able to read people quickly and accurately.
- We both need to be able to ask the right questions to get the information we need.
- We both need to be good listeners to pick up on important clues.
- We both need to have excellent powers of observation to notice small details that could be important.
- We both need excellent memory recall to remember all the details of a case or a sale.
- We both need to be able to think on our feet and come up with creative solutions when faced with a problem.
- We both need strong persuasion skills to convince others of our point of view.
- We both need to be able to handle rejection without taking it personally.
- We both need to be patient to keep working on a case or a sale even when there are no quick results.
- We both need thick skin to deal with the stress and criticism that come with the job.
- We both need to work well under pressure and meet deadlines.
- We both need to be able to stay calm in difficult situations.

- We both need to be good at multitasking and be able to handle multiple cases or sales at the same time.
- We both need to have a strong sense of determination to succeed.
- Finally, we both need to enjoy the challenge that comes with the job and have a passion for what we do.

Solving the Sale Like Sherlock Holmes

Sherlock Holmes was the world's greatest detective because he could observe and deduce the smallest details about people and situations. This skill would have also made him an excellent practitioner of the S^3 method. Holmes would be able to read his clients, understand their needs, and then provide them with a perfect solution just like you will. Holmes was also very persuasive, and while his persuasion was borne of cold deductive reasoning, he was always involved in a case or a crime rooted in passion and emotion.

Likewise, as modern-day detectives, we are piecing together the puzzle of our client's sales predicaments with deduction and logic as our tools. However, we must always remain aware that passion and emotion are at the root. Additionally, Holmes's calm demeanor and ability to think on his feet allowed him to constantly think ahead and plan for every eventuality. Holmes was never caught off guard and could always find the best solution to any problem. We must do the same.

There are many ways to solve problems, but among the most effective ways is to use the same process as Sherlock Holmes. Holmes was known for solving crimes that no one else could solve. You may not solve crimes, but you can become known for pulling off spectacular feats of sales detective work that no one else can accomplish. How did Holmes do it? He applied a process of analysis that helped him break each problem down into smaller pieces so that each of the smaller pieces was easier to solve.

Holmes began by gathering information about the problem. He then looked for patterns and clues in the information he had gathered. By doing this, Holmes could see things other people might not see. He also used his knowledge of human behavior to help him understand what was happening in a situation. After zooming out, as we spoke about before, Holmes would also zoom in on the details of the case to create intense clarity.

Once Holmes analyzed all of the information, he came up with a plan of action, then he took steps to implement his plan and solve the problem. Under the S^3 method, discovery is where we discover our plan of action with the client's input and participation. It works best when there is a "eureka moment" for the client and for us. It doesn't matter who has the eureka moment first. It only matters that both parties get a little exhilarated that an answer has been found that fits the client to a T.

It doesn't matter who has the eureka moment first.

Denouement Ties Up Loose Ends

Now it might seem that after the solution has been found, one is ready to barrel right into the close, but not so fast. In a detective novel, the denouement is the final resolution of the plot. It is the place where the facts of the case are retold, and all of the loose ends of the case are tied up. The definition of denouement per the Encyclopedia Britannica Online is as follows: "denouement (French: 'unknotting') conclusion after the climax of a narrative in which the complexities of the plot are unraveled, and the conflict is finally resolved."

In the denouement, all of the plotlines are tied up. In our case, the client's stated and unstated requirements and desires, logical and emotional motivations, pain points, and everything it takes to solve these issues to the client's satisfaction are evident. This is where the criminal detective reveals who committed the crime or where the lovers finally confess their love for each other. In our case, the eureka moment is when the client realizes they would have to be foolish not to buy what we are selling—but it must be the client arriving at that decision. As we lay out all of the facts of the case, our client discovers how well our solution addresses all of their logical and emotional needs.

Educating, assisting, and, when necessary, leading the client to make their own decision are combined into what we are calling *persuasion* in the next chapter.

Yes, at this point, we may have solved the puzzle and arrived at a solution, but that does not mean we are ready to start signing contracts and ordering delivery. This is a mistake that many salespeople make, that is to say, going for the conclusion of the transaction too soon.

In fact, under the S^3 method, our goal is not to go for anything, but instead to lead our clients into basically closing themselves. They should already know they need to move forward with the transaction, and all they need from us is to walk them through the process.

People love to buy, but they hate being sold. The denouement in the S^3 method is equivalent to making a final proposal or final presentation. It is obvious that to present before you understand the client's needs is an open audition for disaster. Similarly, attempting to complete a transaction before the client knows you thoroughly understand her best interests will most likely be met with mistrust, suspicion, and objections.

It is more common in complex sales to have a series of discovery conversations where information is gathered. Depending on the complexity of the sale, this process could take months, and if you're dealing with the government, this process could take years. Nevertheless, a proposal is not warranted until all of the facts have come in and have been thoroughly verified, analyzed, and verified again.

Now you may be thinking: *What about a short sales cycle? What about a micro-sales cycle?* People come in, buy toothpaste and leave; people call me up, I paint their garage, and I leave; people come in, I clean I straighten their teeth, examine their eyes, take their blood pressure and temperature [fill in the blank for your own short-term sales transaction] and leave. *What can I do about that?*

There, I would answer a question with a question: "How would you like to sell more?" Even if your typical transactions take place so quickly, you don't see how to go through all 7 steps in real life, as that's okay.

Let's do an Einstein Experiment and visualize you and your client going through the entire 7-step process in this book, no matter how clipped or abbreviated your current process really is, even if you're only selling a bag of Skittles or you're that little boy or girl with the sidewalk lemonade stand.

- Walk yourself through what a hidden desire analysis might look like.
- Walk yourself through the various ways to connect with your client more deeply.
- Walk your way through what an imagined exploration of their seen and unseen needs might look like. How does it sound? How does it feel?
- Walk your way through a side-by-side discovery of possible business solutions you've never thought of or considered before now.
- Look for a "eureka moment" when you see something that was hidden but now suddenly seems so obvious.
- Walk through the presentation, the denouement, of the ideal solution answering all the open questions that exist and tying up loose ends.

If you are being thorough, see if you're not seeing more ways to sell, better ways to sell, more ways to get bigger sales more frequently, and ways to better satisfy more customers. Then write me and tell me about it.

Key Takeaways in Chapter 4

- A professional salesperson is like a detective because we are always looking for clues and trying to uncover new information.
- Likewise, as modern-day detectives, we are piecing together the puzzle of our client's sales predicaments with deduction and logic as our tools. However, we must always remain aware that passion and emotion are at the root.
- Under the S^3 method, our goal is not to go for the close, but instead to lead our clients to close themselves after being presented with all of the facts and evidence on a logical and emotional level.

Chapter 5

PERSUASION AND SELECTION

*Character may also be called
the most effective means of persuasion.*
Aristotle

This one's a fun story, and it's all about Christmas time. We're in the throes of Christmas; people are shopping like crazy and enjoying themselves. It's December something or another, and we had been shipped these wire reindeer indoor/outdoor decorations. They were extremely well-made, eye-catching ornaments in two colors, silver and gold, and three different sizes. The large ones were 20", the medium ones were 15," and the small ones were 10." They cost, as I recall, $25, $20, and $15, respectively. They did not have lights, but the mesh portion of the body had glittery designs that somehow made the reindeer look sparkly. We set them up in a display on the sales floor to sell them right out the door as quickly as possible.

The mediums sold the best. The large ones were rather sizable for walking straight out of the door with, but they eventually did go, and the smaller ones, while they looked adorable to me, were the slower ones to sell, but even those went out the door, too. I got one of the small ones for myself.

The curious thing was that everyone bought only the gold ones in all three sizes. No one was buying the silver reindeer in any size. No one. The reindeer proved popular, and it didn't take long to exhaust our entire gold reindeer inventory in a few days. After a few more days, we couldn't even get the gold reindeer from our regional warehouse. This had become a region-wide phenomenon. The region was out of stock on the gold reindeer, but there were plenty of silver reindeers to go around in all sizes.

Customers quickly noticed the gold reindeer were no longer available. Folks would stroll into the store and say, "I remember you had these in reindeer in gold. Do you have any left? I really like the gold ones."

No one was buying the doggone silver ones. No one. Not only could we not get a shipment from the warehouse, but we also couldn't even get the warehouse to give us a possible shipment date; therefore, we had no information to give to our customers other than, "You can have any color you want as long as it's silver." Then it hit me. I decided to have my staff go out, get spray paint, and paint all the silver reindeer inventory gold.

Like a good little manager, I solicited my team for buy-in before executing my evil plot. I called a quick meeting, leaving one person on the sales floor while I gathered the rest together in the back. I said, "Look here, people are buying these reindeer like hotcakes, right? But they're only buying the gold ones, am I correct?" Without hesitation, everyone said or nodded, "Yes."

So, I continued, "We've seen for a few days now nobody wants the silver, and people are coming in asking for the gold reindeer, am I right? Once again, they all agreed, though someone added, "But the silver ones are kind of pretty." "Yes," I said, "They're pretty, but they aren't pretty enough for people to buy them. I am going to give you all some money out of petty cash, and you're all going to go out and take turns buying spray paint from the hardware store. Then you are all going to go to the back of the store and start painting all of these silver son-of-a-guns GOLD."

I can't really describe the look they all gave me at first. It looked like how you might look on those mornings when you wake up and, for a split second, you're not sure exactly where you are. *Am I still in a dream? Am I in my own bed? I'm not sure.* They were probably thinking, *Has she gone off her rocker? How long before my shift is over? Can I avoid her until then?*

So, I sent out my stock manager, Kareem, and I said, "Kareem, when you pick up the spray paint, also see if you can find some gold glitter."

He goes, "Gold glitter?"

I said, "Yes, after you spray paint them, I want you to sprinkle them with glitter, so maybe they will look like they're sparkling."

"Look like they are sparkling. Right. Are you kidding me?"

"No," I explained. And I added, "One more thing. Make sure you buy lots of cardboard we can put underneath the reindeer while spray painting them."

Kareem goes out the back door, all the while saying, "This is crazy. I'll do it. But this is crazy. You're going to owe me for this one."

Once I got the stock manager to do it, I figured everyone else would fall in line. Kareem came back in about 20 minutes with three cans of spray paint. The spray paint was an old gold color close to the original gold reindeer color but not an exact match. I still had the little one I had bought in the back so that I could compare. Anyway, I figured it was close enough if there was nothing else around to compare it against.

"Okay, did you get the glitter?" I asked.

"Yes, I got the glitter."

"Okay then, we're going to start with a couple of medium ones. Take them out back and spray paint the heck out of them. Be sure to lay the cardboard down first, so we're not spray painting the sidewalk." I sent Kareem out back and sent the next person out to buy more spray paint and gold glitter.

It's Christmas time in New York, so it was cold outside. I had the whole team out there spray painting and glittering like bandits. They were outside grumbling and complaining while I was inside selling. Once we had a half dozen finished, I let everyone stop there so we could let them dry overnight. In the morning, we would put them on the floor and see how it all goes.

The following day, we put them on the sales floor, and sure enough, those doggone reindeer were gone in a couple of hours.

I said, "Okay. We're spraying the whole lot. Get out there and get going."

They said, "That's like 24 reindeer."

I'm like, "Yes. We're spray painting every size."

"Are you kidding me?"

"No." We sprayed painted all those little suckers and sold them all in a few days.

Every other Tuesday afternoon, there is a regional conference where all the managers go over their numbers. Everybody gets to hear what everyone else has done—the good, the bad, and the hideous sometimes. The numbers showed that my store had sold all of its silver reindeer. Everyone was stunned.

"You must tell us how you sold the silver reindeer because everybody seems to be on the gold. What did you do that got the silver to sell?"

I said, "Well, do you want me to tell you?"

They said, "Yes, of course, we want you to tell us."

"Are you sure you really want to hear this?"

"C'mon, Ruth, give already."

And so, I told them the story about spray painting all of the reindeer and covering them with gold glitter.

They said, "Are you kidding us?"

"No. I am not kidding you. To keep the inventory straight, they went out of the door with the silver product tags, but they were golden and glittery when they left the store."

That was like the shot heard around the world. Everyone had sold out of their silver reindeer by the next regional sales call.

When we sold the last one, I remember it wasn't even completely dry. After the lady who wanted it pointed this out, we walked her up to the register, and I snatched that little rascal off the floor and crammed it into the employee bathroom. I started running a hair dryer across it like a mad woman, like I was reenacting an episode of *I Love Lucy.* Doing everything I could to get the damp spots dry enough to go out the door."

Someone came back and said, "She's ready to go."

"I'm not ready yet. You have to stall her."

"How am I supposed to do that?"

"I don't know, try to sell her a Santa Claus or something. It's Christmas, for crying out loud." Anyway, as the lady walked out the door, I remember the reindeer still smelled like wet paint.

That was only one of many close calls over the years. But sometimes, you have to improvise, adapt, and overcome to satisfy the client. Innovating to meet the market's demand is essential in a capitalistic society. All in all, the client made a selection, and we honored that selection. Instead of saying, "You can have any color you want as long as it's silver," we said, "Stay right there for a moment, please, while I step into the back room."

Persuasion is a Ballet, not an MMA Match

When it comes to persuasion, some people have two left feet while others are as graceful as if they should be on *Dancing with the Stars*. If you are more like the latter, then you know persuasion can be much like dancing.

With the right teacher and practice, anyone can become a good dancer or master the delicate art of influence. But even if you're not born a dancer or a persuasion expert, that doesn't mean you can't learn. For one, both require a certain amount of skill and natural ability.

Another similarity between dancing and persuasion is that both require understanding your partner. In dancing, you need to understand your partner's steps and movements in order to flow together seamlessly. In persuasion, you need to understand your customer's needs and wants in order to offer the perfect solution.

If the solution truly is perfect, it should require minimal persuasion, if any.

Finally, dancing and persuasion are all about connecting with your partner. Whether on the dance floor or in the sales process, the goal is always to create a rapport and build a relationship. The better you understand your customer and the stronger the connection you make, the more persuasive you will be. After all, people are more likely to buy from someone they like and trust.

Just as a dance routine must be practiced and rehearsed before it can be performed flawlessly, a sales plan must be carefully crafted and executed to be persuasive. To create a persuasive sales plan, you need to consider all the elements that will come together to create the final product offering, i.e., your products or services, your target market, your competition, your pricing strategy, your sales process, and more. Each of these elements must be carefully coordinated to create a solution that satisfies the stated need and goes one step further.

Like a good dance routine, a well-executed sales plan can be a thing of beauty. When everything comes together perfectly, it can be a joy to watch (or participate in). Just as a poorly executed dance routine can be cringeworthy, so, too, can a sales plan that is not well thought out and executed.

This is exactly why if you've followed the process meticulously up until now in collaboration with your client, you have already fit all of the pieces into a beautiful picture puzzle of the client's desired outcome. Educating, assisting, and, when necessary, leading the client to make their own decision is what we are calling persuasion.

Persuasion isn't bludgeoning your client's will into submission no matter how subtly and unobtrusively you might be able to pull it off. Nothing is more persuasive than what the heart already wants. You only need to find that, and it will lead you to their dreams.

Nothing is more persuasive than what the heart already wants.

Persuasion Changes Over Time

The theme of this book is that once your outside self fully aligns with everything you need to do on the inside to demonstrate sales mastery, you will, at that moment, be a master. When you build from the inside out, mastery is not only possible; it is inevitable. We learn techniques only to the point where we internalize them. Once the techniques are fully internalized, they are no longer techniques but have become part of our being.

I thought it might be interesting to run through a brief history of modern thoughts about the art and science of persuasion. Techniques of persuasion have evolved to become more sophisticated and effective. For example, in ancient times, people used simple methods such as emotional appeals and flattery to try to convince others.

Theories of persuasion before 1950 were dominated by the concept of direct, explicit persuasion. This approach to persuasion assumes that people are rational creatures who make decisions based on carefully considering all available information. The persuader's goal was simply to provide additional information that would sway the decision-maker in the desired direction.

However, this view of human nature has been increasingly challenged in recent years. A growing body of research suggests that people are often irrational and emotional in their decision-making, and direct persuasion is often ineffective. Instead, persuasive strategies that focus on indirect influence may be more effective.

In the 1950s and 1960s, theories of persuasion focused on the effects of messages on individuals, with little attention paid to the context in which those messages were received. In the 1970s and onwards, theories of persuasion began to consider how people process information and how information processing affected their response to persuasive messages.

In the early 1980s, most persuasion theories focused on cognitive processes, such as information processing and decision-making. Social cognition theories dominated the field, with the elaboration of the likelihood model being one of the most influential. This model proposed two main routes to persuasion: the central route, which is based on careful thought and consideration of the message, and the peripheral route, which is based on more superficial cues, such as the source's attractiveness or credibility.

Theory and research in persuasion began to shift in the late 1980s and early 1990s, and the power of emotions became increasingly recognized and studied as an essential factor in persuasion. More research began to examine specific aspects of how emotions could influence attitudes and behavior.

Neuroscience has been around for centuries, but it wasn't until recently that it was applied to the world of sales. Neuroscience is the study of the nervous system and covers everything from how individual cells work, how the brain processes information, and how we move and feel emotions. In the early 1990s, researchers began to study how the brain works when someone is making a purchase decision. This research has led to many new techniques for selling products and services.

One of the most important discoveries made by neuroscientists is that people are not rational beings. Our brains are hardwired to make decisions based on emotions, not logic. This means you must appeal to the customer's emotions, not just their intellect, when trying to sell them something.

Another thing researchers have learned about the brain is that it's very good at remembering emotionally charged things. That's why creating a positive emotional connection with your customers is crucial if you want them to remember your product or service.

Neuroscientists have been working to understand how the brain processes information during sales interactions and how this information can be used to improve sales outcomes. Some of the most critical findings from this research include the following:

- The brain constantly processes information about the environment, including potential threats and opportunities. This information processing occurs at an unconscious level outside of our conscious awareness. Salespeople who can effectively read and respond to these unconscious cues from their customers (uncovered motives and hidden desires) are more likely to be successful in sales interactions.

- The brain is wired to pay more attention to negative than positive information. This negativity bias can lead salespeople to focus too much on the potential for failure in a sales interaction and not enough on the potential for success. Salespeople who can reframe their thinking to focus on the positive aspects of a sales interaction are more likely to be successful.

- Our brains are wired to seek out social approval from others. This need for social approval can lead salespeople to make decisions that are not in their best interest, such as agreeing to unreasonable customer demands. Salespeople who are aware of this tendency and work to resist it are more likely to be successful in negotiations.

- Sales is an ever-changing field, and neuroscience is providing new insights that can help salespeople be more successful. Neuroscientists are studying how people make decisions, and this research is being used to develop new sales strategies. For example, neuroscientists have found that people are more likely to purchase if they feel a connection to the salesperson. This finding has led to new sales techniques focusing on building rapport with potential customers.

- Neuroscientists have also found that people are more likely to trust a salesperson if they believe that the salesperson is like them. This finding has led to developing new sales strategies that focus on establishing common ground with potential customers. As neuroscience continues to advance, it is likely that salespeople will increasingly use neuroscience-based techniques to improve their success.

When you build it from the inside out, sales mastery is not only possible—it is inevitable.

When the Solution Is So Obvious, It Must Be Selected

Steve Martin, the comedian, has been known to give the advice, "Be so good they can't ignore you." I know it's difficult to explain exactly how you go about doing that. All the same, the step-by-step instructions on how you would go about doing that will depend upon what it is you're actually doing.

What is far more important than any step-by-step instructions (that will necessarily change over time) is the mindset and desire that drives you towards committing to do whatever it takes to make yourself so good that you can't be ignored. Likewise, in sales, careful analysis and research, solid connections with the clients, crafting a sales strategy and solution that fits each client's needs like no other creates a solution so obvious your client should willingly select it.

You may have noticed up to this point, I haven't said anything about costs or pricing issues as part of the sale solution. Certainly, money will always be an important consideration. I've seen this quote attributed to several people, "Money might not be the most important thing, but it's right up there with air." Suffice it to say that if the client handed you a dollar and you handed the client two dollars, the client would be giving you dollars all day and all night. In mastering sales, your focus must always be on delivering at least significant value to the client—overwhelming value is even better. Adopt the philosophy that price is not the problem, and it will serve you well.

Figure 5. Cost is a real objection only if perceived value is not clear

If there are multiple alternatives in your proposal, that is fine. Everyone feels empowered by the opportunity to make a selection. However, we know from decision science and marketing psychology that offering too many choices can backfire and cause indecision. When asked the question how many options are too many, three always seems to be the optimal number of alternatives suggested. Nevertheless, the best option for the client among several viable options should be as obvious as possible for legitimate reasons. It is still true that a confused mind always says, "No." When the solution is clear, and clearly superior to all other alternatives, then an agreement can be reached with minimal fuss and fanfare.

The solution should be so blindingly obvious to everyone that one of two things happens. Either the client asks you, "So what are our next steps?" or you say to the client, "Here's what we're going to need to do next." Then the next steps flow as naturally as if you were doing synchronized swimming.

If, for some reason, that is not the case, then continue asking questions and gathering information until you feel confident you understand and your client understands that you understand their needs, both stated and unspoken.

This cannot be stressed enough. If, at this point, you are still receiving any resistance on the client's part, this is not necessarily a bad thing. If the client has withheld information, if you've been unable to dredge deeply enough below the surface to find the desire that sparks the emotion that leads the client to make a favorable decision for your product or service, that might be the best outcome of all. That could very well be a reason to continue the celebration.

Let's face it, we live in the real world. Time and circumstances are always factors. Needs change, personalities change, and it's far better to walk away with all of the investment everyone has made during the sales conversation intact. Clients do sometimes come back. In classic sales training in the past, salespeople were trained that there is no tomorrow. Clients have too many opportunities to find alternate solutions in today's world and certainly tomorrow, so yesterday's hard-sell techniques no longer apply, and they will insult people if you try them.

Once again, if you've reached this point and the solution is not obvious, you can continue the sales conversation by asking more questions. Here are a few reasons why continued questioning is so critical to completing the sales process:

1. Questioning helps you understand your customer's needs. The better you understand them, the better you can serve them.
2. Asking questions allows you to get to the root of their problem and identify the best solution for them.

3. Questioning shows that you're genuinely invested in helping your client.

4. Continuing to ask questions, even at this point in the process, shows that you care about finding the right solution for your client. It shows that you're not just trying to sell them something as you are genuinely interested in helping them.

5. Continuing to ask questions at this point continues to build rapport.

6. Building and strengthening rapport doesn't have a time limit, and it doesn't have an end. If there is anyone in your life you don't think you need to continue to build rapport with, I encourage you to think again. Always be connecting.

7. Questioning helps you overcome objections. Objections are a natural part of the sales process. But, by asking questions, you can uncover and/or overcome them and move closer to consummation and celebration.

If you are dealing with commodities where everyone essentially sells the same widget, these are traditionally price-sensitive, price-dominated environments, and that is a fact. However, even in these situations, sales masters prevail against their competition and retain valuable customers because they offer something that can never be commoditized. They *connect* with their clients on a deeper level.

They've taken the time to uncover hidden desires, invested in time and money to foster deep connections with the client and the client's organization, been unflinching in their exploration of the client's deepest motivations, and done the detective work and presented all of the logical and emotional reasons why, even in an environment where everyone's product appears to be the same, they are still providing an unmatched value, even if that value is their demonstrable commitment to unmatched value. But it has to be demonstrated.

The bottom line is that when you've set everything up so that the solutions and alternatives are obvious to everyone involved, there is nothing more to do than help the client complete their selection. Let the satisfaction begin.

Always Be Connecting.

Key Takeaways in Chapter 5

- There are many similarities between dancing and persuasion. Both require understanding and matching your partner's steps and movements to flow together seamlessly.

- In persuasion, you need to understand your customer's needs and wants in order to offer the perfect solution.

- Cost is a meaningful objection only if the overwhelming value has not been established.

- Researchers have learned that the brain is very good at remembering emotionally charged things. That's why creating a positive emotional connection with your customers is crucial if you want them to remember your product or service.

SATISFY THE DREAM

Chapter 6

CONSUMMATION: YES, I SAID IT.

*Remember, the most difficult tasks are consummated
not by a single explosive burst of energy or effort
but by the constant daily application
of the best you have within you.*
Og Mandino

O ne of the things that you pick up on quickly in the retail clothing industry is that you've got to watch what's going on in the dressing rooms. A lot of shoplifting goes on in there. If you don't keep your eye on it, bad things will happen. Every now and then, someone might lose their balance, hit one of the walls, or fall down. You just knock on the door and say, "Are you okay in there?" They usually just let you know they're all right.

When you're dealing with the public all day long, seven days a week, anything can and does happen. We've had people fall down, pass out, and call for help where we've had to call the police or 911. I've also had, a couple of times, a situation where noises were going on in the dressing room that didn't sound like a woman struggling to put on a pair of boots. I've knocked on a dressing room door more than once and heard the frantic fumbling and rumbling sound of two people trying to get dressed in a hurry. As usual, one voice blurts out, "Um. Just a minute."

Yes. I have run across people who have decided the fitting room inside a retail clothing store would be the perfect place to get it on. How classy. How romantic. Anyway, that's not the kind of consummation I'm about to talk about. But obviously, I chose the word on purpose, while understanding all its connotations.

Consumer has the same root as consummate.

On the other hand, I don't think it is an accident that we talk about sales relationships and engagements, and I also don't believe it is a coincidence that *consumer* has the same root as *consummate.* Consummation is the part of the sales process where the parties come together to satisfy the union for which they both have a desire.

I chose consummation because, at this stage of the process, a master handles the post-close with as much care and delicacy as laying a newborn baby to bed.

A master handles the post-close with as much care and delicacy as laying a newborn baby to bed.

THE CONSUMMATION TRIAD
FIRST STAGE OF POST-CLOSING

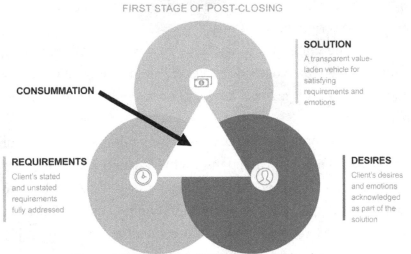

SOLUTION
A transparent value-laden vehicle for satisfying requirements and emotions

CONSUMMATION

REQUIREMENTS
Client's stated and unstated requirements fully addressed

DESIRES
Client's desires and emotions acknowledged as part of the solution

Figure 6. The Immutable Triad of Closing is a solution that satisfies client's requirements, desires, and emotions

Closing Should Be a Foregone Conclusion

Having clients say, "Shut up and take my money," is the position I'm always going for. You should have been hearing that by the end of the last chapter.

So, let's be clear that where we are right now is the post-closing process and really the first phase of post-closing. We're wrapping up the sale in the first post-closing phase and arranging for any needed follow-up. We're celebrating the sale and setting up future business in the second post-closing phase.

In a complex sale, this process can take months. This is often where legal departments get involved with re-reading and red-lining contracts. The Purchasing Department from the other side wakes up and says, "Holy crap! You can't do that (buy that product or service) without going through us first. Tear up all that paperwork. We're going to make you go through everything right from the beginning. Call us back next month as we're too busy for you right now anyway."

Then the client has to escalate up the chain of command, and some VP from your side has to call some VP from their side and...*Oh, I'm sorry. I was having a post-traumatic sales disorder attack.*

You'll never encounter any issues or landmines during your post-close. That never happens, right? Wrong. Even on a less complex level, it could be a credit app or even a credit card that gets disapproved. The consummation process isn't always as flawless as we might like, but remember part of our job is to think ahead and be prepared for any eventuality. Like a groom stumbling over the threshold, it's not the stumble, it's the recovery.

I'd like you to play a game with me for a second. This might require some thinking on your part, or it may not. I want you to remember the best salesperson and best sales experience you've ever had. It doesn't matter when, where, what item, or how much the item cost. It could have been a suit, a watch, a pair of shoes, a house, a boat, a car. Well, probably not a car—just kidding.

But you get the point; it's not the item or service that matters. It's the fact that you remembered the salesperson you worked with. How did they greet you? How did they build rapport? How did they ask questions and probe for details?

I love being in the hands of a master salesperson, and I've enjoyed the experience of working with masterful salespeople many times. I wish every time I was out to buy something, I had the good fortune to be handled by a master of the art.

How did they answer your questions and concerns? Did they handle your objections, or were they pleasant and courteous as they helped you sort out your real concerns from an unfortunate lack of information? Did they close you? Did they even need to?

What do you remember the most about the experience overall with that particular person? You remember how they made you feel. Isn't that, right? That's what I call *high resonance.*

Resonance results from matching the client's needs and the seller's offering. When there is resonance, the client and seller feel a connection, and the client is more likely to buy.

You generate resonance as you probe for your client's desires. Your resonant nature helps clients to open up. You generate resonance while you are forming a connection. Resonance increases the strength of your connection as you continue through the engagement. As you explore possibilities and mutually discover the solution to the client's problem, resonance builds as you make your presentation, reaching a crescendo at the point of selection.

Even after this peak experience at the point of selection, resonance must not be left to go on autopilot. That would be a huge mistake. Resonance must still be cultivated and made to increase long after the sale. Continuing resonance is the path to repeat business.

When there is resonance, the client feels they understand what the seller is saying and can trust them. This connection makes the sales engagement go more smoothly and increases the chances of getting a positive outcome on both sides.

Creating resonance is not always easy, but it is essential to your mastery. When clients and sellers connect on a deep level, both parties benefit. The client gets what they need and the seller achieves their mission of satisfying the client's need.

Satisfying the Dream

We all share the common desire to be happy and fulfilled no matter our individual hopes and dreams. We all want to experience love, success, and adventure in our lives. We can make our lives more meaningful and enjoyable by working towards our goals and striving to make our dreams a reality.

If you can imagine for a second, maybe your product or service and even you are not so important to a client's life. Then, when you look beyond what you're trying to sell and really look into the life your client wants to live, if you're not very careful, you may stumble across one or many of your client's dreams.

How can you know a person's dreams? Of course, the obvious and immensely unsatisfying answer would be just to ask. But assuming that this kind of direct question is rarely appropriate in a typical sales conversation, you and I can still do our very best to surmise.

There's no one answer to the question since everyone has different dreams and aspirations. However, according to a study by Harris Interactive, the top 10 dreams of the average person are:

1. Travel the world
2. Fall in love and get married
3. Be successful in their career
4. Live a healthy lifestyle
5. Buy a home
6. Raise a family

7. Retire comfortably
8. Give back to the community
9. Experience new cultures
10. Be happy

While some of these dreams may be universal, others are specific to an individual's goals and desires. Yet, with that list as a starting point, a little active listening and deductive reasoning could take you a long way towards gaining a next-level perspective on your client.

Satisfaction Guaranteed

When it comes to satisfying customers, there is no room for error. This is why it is also essential in today's uncertain world to satisfy the client and ensure that satisfaction is guaranteed. There are a few standard types of guarantees you and your company might provide:

1. Performance Guarantee: This guarantee states that the seller will perform as agreed upon in the contract. This could include things like delivering the product on time or fixing any errors that may occur.
2. Payment Guarantee: This guarantee ensures that the client will pay for the product or service as agreed upon in the contract. This can help to reduce any risk on behalf of the seller.
3. Delivery Guarantee: This guarantee promises that the product or service will be delivered on time and in the proper condition.

A guarantee gives customers peace of mind, knowing they can get their money back if they aren't happy with the purchase, or they can get help from the company if there are any problems with the product or service. For businesses, a guarantee can help reduce the risk of returning products or dealing with unhappy customers. If you cannot offer any other type of guarantee, then guarantee your client that you will always be there.

When you make the personal guarantee that you will always be there for your client, it means there will be at least 20 other things you will have to do:

1. Exceed expectations
2. Go the extra mile
3. Follow up
4. Personalize the experience
5. Build relationships
6. Resolve issues quickly and effectively
7. Be proactive
8. Listen to feedback
9. Take responsibility
10. Communicate openly and honestly
11. Be dependable
12. Have a positive attitude
13. Offer incentives
14. Show appreciation
15. Provide exceptional customer service
16. Deliver on promises
17. Don't oversell
18. Educate your customers

19. Be human
20. Strive to create a raving fan

When it comes to what clients value most from a salesperson, there are many different opinions. However, after conducting research and interviewing several clients, the following three qualities emerged as the most important:

First, clients appreciate honesty and integrity. Sales professionals must always be truthful with their clients or trust will quickly be lost.

Second, clients appreciate someone who is knowledgeable and can provide expert advice. Salespeople need to stay up to date on the latest industry trends and be able to share this information with their clients.

Third, clients appreciate someone who is responsive and provides prompt service. If a client has a question or needs help with something, they expect to receive a quick response from the salesperson. That's all part of your commitment to sales mastery

Key Takeaways: Chapter 6

- Closing should be a foregone conclusion. The goal of the S^3 method is having clients say, "Shut up and take my money."

- High intention, high clarity and high resonance are essential to the sales process; however, resonance should be fostered long after the sale.

- We must not only satisfy but do everything we can to make sure satisfaction is guaranteed.

- What clients appreciate most are honesty and integrity, up-to-date knowledge and experience and prompt customer service. Our mastery of sales requires unwavering excellence in all of the above.

Chapter 7

CELEBRATION

*Learn to celebrate every moment of your life and
you will find more and more reasons to celebrate life.*
Purvi Raniga

T he way that I knew I was good as a salesperson was that clients kept coming back. Women and men would return to tell me how they enjoyed wearing something or using something I'd sold to them. They brought in friends, gave me referrals, brought presents, and showed me pictures of their families. It was clear to me from the very beginning that selling offered the potential for not only a rewarding career with extraordinary income potential but also that selling was an opportunity to connect beyond the normal, everyday, superficial experiences.

As Isabelle said, "If you want to eat off of paper plates every day, that's fine. You can do that." I am saying if you want every interaction with another human being to be an experience no more significant than a paper plate, that's fine. You can do that.

But I must believe that if you are reading this book, you want something more. You want to be a master at something and everything that it entails. You want to be a master at sales, which we should agree by now is somewhere along the spectrum of highly significant vocations. Like a doctor who heals bodies, a psychiatrist who heals minds, and a priest who heals souls, salespeople heal wants, and salespeople heal needs, and at the highest level, salespeople help clients fulfill their dreams. Take your work that seriously, and you will be that serious a professional and that serious of an asset to humanity. Just sayin'.

It doesn't matter how small your job is or how small you think it is. It also doesn't matter what your job is or how big you think it may be. If you would take every moment of this life, the one and only life you have right now, and make it something that you are willing to celebrate, it will change your life in the twinkle of an eye.

If you would take every moment of this life, the one and only life you have right now, and make it something that you are willing to celebrate, it will change your life in the twinkle of an eye.

Sitting down to write about celebration, the word *celebrity* came to mind. I thought it might be interesting to mention a few of the celebrities I've run across in some of the places I've worked in the luxury market.

The word *celebrity* is derived from the Latin word *celebritatis*, which means "to be well-known." The English word *celebrity* was first used in the early 1500s and meant "a notable person." Celebrities are people who are famous or well-known for their achievements in a particular field. In the past, celebrities were typically people who were famous for their accomplishments in the arts, such as musicians, actors, and writers. However, in recent years, celebrities have also become known for their accomplishments in other fields, such as business and sports.

I've come across countless numbers of people who fit that description. Just living in New York, where you might see a handful of celebrities on any given day in Manhattan. I am usually not a star-struck person, but I was totally star-struck after running into Calvin Klein. I was a babbling idiot, but I'm sure celebrities get used to that.

With Nina Ricci, I traveled all over the country outfitting department stores with our jewelry line and training the sales staff. I had a team of two other women; we'd all work together in a store or split up and work independently, depending on the circumstances.

I was in Chicago and just finished setting up Neiman Marcus, and I was moving on to Bloomingdale's when I caught wind of the fact that Oprah Winfrey might be visiting the grand opening of the Bloomingdale store downtown as part of one of her events. I headed to the new store and made sure I had everything set up. I was hoping she might somehow come by my counter. I even picked out several pieces especially for Oprah. Sure enough, she came into the store with a considerable entourage.

Before I knew it, the entourage swept right past me, and I barely caught a glimpse. Only a quick flash.

After all that effort and preparation, I felt like this kid in a movie I remember from long ago. This kid chased his favorite star all over the city. I don't remember now if he ever caught up with the star or not. There were a couple of other times I almost caught up with her Oprahness—I'm still going to keep trying.

As a quick aside, I did get interviewed for the *Robb Report,* one of those magazines where if you have to ask the price you can't afford it. They did a feature about the appeal of costume jewelry. I was the national sales manager for one of the top brands. Even though I had a little teeny-weenie quote within the article, it felt pretty darn special to me at the time.

When asked a question by the reporter, I said, "You know, many people want to wear their fine jewelry, but they won't wear it to certain events because if something happens, they might lose it. So, they would rather wear a knockoff and not worry about losing $200, $300, or even $400 worth of jewelry as opposed to losing $10,000 worth of jewelry in a single evening." As I said, it wasn't much. Just my own 15 milliseconds of fame.

I once helped David McCallum, co-star of *The Man from U.N.C.L.E.* and *NCIS* fame. He was gracious and lovely.

I sold dinnerware to Gordon Ramsay; he was an incredibly nice and friendly person. I didn't see any of the shenanigans he's famous for on British and American television.

I had the occasion to sell fine porcelain to Renee Russo. She was no nonsense and knew precisely what she wanted, and I am sure she was happy when we were all done.

I have a very cherished memory of Diahann Carroll when she came into my store. She was an actress perhaps best known for her starring role as Julia Baker, a nurse, and single mother, in the television series *Julia* from 1968 to 1971. As a television show, *Julia* was groundbreaking as it showed a woman of color in a contemporary setting in a professional role instead of as a maid or a nanny. The show tackled controversial topics such as interracial relationships and abortion. Critics praised *Julia* for its realistic portrayal of the African Americans' experiences. She was the first Black woman to have her own television series, for which she also won a Golden Globe Award. A versatile performer, she was in dozens of stage and screen productions. She had numerous large and small roles in television, including co-starring roles in series like *Dynasty, Grey's Anatomy,* and *White Collar.*

Yet, on top of that, from 1969 to1972, Mattel Toys produced a Barbie-sized Julia Doll, and guess who had one of those as a little girl growing up. How often do you meet and interact with someone you watched on TV every week and played with them as a doll? Come on now.

I was working for Mikasa at the time. It was a typical day, and I was in a typical daydream until I heard someone whisper, "Is that Diahann Carroll?" I went over to look, and sure enough, it was Diahann Carroll, and she was all by herself, or at least she had come into the store by herself. So, I went over to her and asked if there was anything I could help her with, and she said no, just looking around. So, I went about my business, no big deal. It's just Julia walking around in my store. No big deal. Nope. None at all.

She was looking at some very high-end crystal. Great product. She also showed interest in dinnerware designed by Oscar de la Renta. The staff and I left her alone and let her take her time. When she was ready to check out, she'd selected a pair of gorgeous crystal candle sticks. So, I was behind the register ringing her up. I took her candlesticks and painstakingly wrapped them up and carefully boxed them.

Once I was done, she said to me, "But there's one thing that I need," and I'm like, "Okay, what else can we help you with?" She said, "I need them gift wrapped."

Total silence. We look at each other. We never did gift wrapping at this store. I didn't say that. Instead, I said, "What type of gift wrapping would you need?"

"They're going to be a wedding gift."

Going to be a wedding gift. Okay.

I took a deep breath and said, "Well, we'll be happy to do that for you. But it won't be ready for a while, maybe about 45 minutes to an hour. Will that work for you?"

She smiled just a little and said, "Oh, yes. I'll be shopping in the mall; I can come back in an hour, no worries."

"That's great. See you in a little while."

She walked out the door. Here I was again about to pull off another caper. Fortunately for me, gift-wrapping is a big hobby of mine. I knew I could gift-wrap with the best of them. That wasn't the problem. The problem was that since the store never did gift-wrapping, I had no materials to work with. I didn't even know where I was going to find all of the gift-wrapping materials I would need. I had no idea if I could pull this off in 58 minutes and counting.

I pulled my team together, "Look, somebody's got to go out and find some wrapping paper and ribbons right away,"

"But we don't do gift-wrapping,"

"Well, we're gift-wrapping something up today, and we've got to get it done in less than an hour,"

"This is crazy." *Where have I heard that before?*

Shelly looked the least confused and resistant out of the three of them.

"Okay, Shelly, I'm going to give you some cash. You need to go out, find a drugstore and get some wrapping paper for a wedding gift. I'm also going to need a white or silver ribbon with a big fluffy white or silver bow,"

"Can't you just do it while we watch the store?"

"No, I'm the only manager on duty. I can't leave the store. We've only got 50 minutes left; get out of here."

Shelly marched off but didn't make it back for over 30 minutes, which seemed like an eternity. I only had 20 minutes left. Anyway, the paper looked fine, and Shelly found everything I needed, thank God. I ran into the back office and gift-wrapped the thing like a hibachi chef, with shreds of ribbon and wrapping paper flying all over the place. I got it done with five minutes to sparc. I put a nice fluffy bow on top; it came out great. I took it back out front to the counter and placed it beside a Mikasa shopping bag.

Just then, I thought, *Oh heck. We don't have a gift card for her to sign.* Too late, she was just walking through the door. She came up to the counter and asked to see it. I pulled it out of the bag to show it to her, and she said, "Oh, that's fine. That will do."

And I'm like, "Okay, that'll do. That's fine. All right, good."

Off she went, and we all said, "Goodbye. Thank you for shopping with us. Hope to see you again soon." Another close shave, and I hate shaving.

I used to have the Turkish prime minister as a regular client, who always came in with her five daughters. She often bought all of her daughters gifts and dinnerware sets, and she would occasionally even send me gifts as well.

There were so many other celebrities in the business, politics, entertainment, and professional sports areas who are too numerous to mention. I can say that to me all of these people were just outstanding. They appreciated the time, energy, and special care you took in assisting them. I was appreciative and thankful for being able to meet them, help them, and get something they really wanted and appreciated. And the exchange was even more enjoyable because they knew, as I knew, they were not just buying an item at that end of the scale; they were usually buying an investment that would serve them well for years to come.

Treat Them Like a Movie Star

By the time we are done with our sales conversation, our clients should feel like they are striding along the velvety red carpet walk of fame on their way to the Oscars. That's the goal. Treat every client, no matter how small, as if they are a million-dollar customer, a world-famous celebrity. But by the way, you should also feel like you are a million-dollar sales professional and a world-famous celebrity in your own right. Then the conversation is one world-famous celebrity to another rather than a glisten-eyed, adoring fan reaching out with a notepad and a pen.

So, you say, "That's wonderful, Ruth, but how exactly am I supposed to do that?" Well, let's try another little Einstein Thought Experiment. Let's just imagine that you are a world-famous celebrity or just a celebrity in your own right. Maybe no one really knows it when you walk out in the street, but in the field of your endeavor, you are a recognized mega-rock star. Put that one on and see how it feels. We're just pretending; it's only a game. Just go with it for a second. Let the feeling wash over you; you're a world-renowned celebrity at the top of your game. Forget about money, notoriety, critics, competition, obligations, clothes, cars, mansions, jewelry, or anything else but the feeling of who you are deep inside and all you've accomplished so far. You feel good. You feel at peace with yourself and the world for one tiny little moment. Just hang on to that for a second.

Now imagine the other person feels exactly the same way about themselves already.

In that mindset, in that mental and spiritual space, have a conversation with them, have a conversation about anything. It doesn't matter what you say so much as it matters that the feeling of celebrity, the feeling of being a celebrated individual, radiates from inside of you to them and radiates back from them to you.

It doesn't matter what you say so much as it matters that the feeling of celebrity, the feeling of being a celebrated individual, radiates from inside of you to them and radiates back from them to you.

Some people may be saying, "Now, come on. This is way out there." No, it's not. I'll prove it to you. Go to YouTube, pull up any two of your favorite celebrities in any profession, and see if you can find an interview where they are given a chance to converse with one another. You'll see what I'm talking about with your own eyes. For the rest of us, you already know what I'm talking about.

How you get there in your unique, precise journey through life is up to you. Once you get there and do what it takes to stay there, your dreams will come true because you've learned to love, enjoy, and master the art of making other people's dreams come true.

Your dreams will come true because you've learned to love, enjoy, and master the art of making other people's dreams come true.

Key Takeaways in Chapter 7

- You are the star of your life. Your customers are the stars of their lives. Each interaction should have the energy of two celebrities engaged in a cordial conversation.
- By the time we are done with our sales conversation, our clients should feel like they are striding along the velvety red carpet walk of fame on their way to the Oscars.
- Committing yourself to the spirit of celebration can change your life in the twinkle of an eye.

Chapter 8

A VISION FOR YOUR FUTURE

*I want every day to be a fresh start
on expanding what is possible.*
Oprah Winfrey

Fifty years of professional selling has allowed me to condense the heart and soul of sales mastery into a simple indirect formula that can be applied to the most complex, multi-phase, technical solution selling there is, right down to the kid's sidewalk lemonade stand in the summertime. The See-Solve-Satisfy (S^3) method has 7 components: desire, connection, expiration, discovery, selection, consummation, and celebration. All components are involved in every phase of selling, no matter how massive or minuscule the transaction.

The goal of the S^3 method and its 7 components is to take you far below the superficial aspect of the typical sales transaction right down to the heart and soul of what really takes place. The transfer of value and service from one human being to another is the essence of life.

Achieving mastery in sales is a high calling. You are signal calling and architecting the transference of energy and emotion. The implications of this power transcend the ringing of a cash register (physically or virtually), a sales quota, a profit-and-loss statement, or a commission check.

When you understand the true power you're holding in your hands, you understand that sales mastery is more than just making a living; it's more than just getting by.

My vision for you is that you now thrive in the oldest profession known to humankind and become free to enjoy all of your dreams no matter what economic conditions may unfold in the future as you commit to satisfying the dreams of others.

The transfer of value and service from one human being to another is the essence of life. Achieving mastery in sales is a high calling. You are signal calling and architecting the transference of energy and emotion.

The Future of Selling

The future of selling is digital and interactive. Customers want to shop online, engage with brands through social media, and receive personalized service. To stay ahead of the competition, retailers need to focus on providing a seamless omnichannel experience for their customers. To create a seamless omnichannel experience, retailers must focus on providing a consistent customer experience across all channels. This means having a strong online presence, being active on social media, and offering convenient shipping and return options. In addition, sales organizations need to make sure their employees are knowledgeable about the products they sell and provide excellent customer service. By providing a positive customer experience, organizations can build brand loyalty and keep customers coming back for more.

Creating a loyal customer base is essential for any business. Not only does it provide you with a reliable source of income, but it also spreads the word about your company and builds up a positive reputation. One of the best ways to create loyal customers is to provide them with positive experiences. This could include anything from providing excellent customer service to offering high-quality products or services. If you can consistently provide your customers with positive experiences, then they are much more likely to remain loyal to your brand. In turn, this will help to boost your sales and profits over the long term.

The future of e-commerce looks equally as exciting. The industry is continuing to grow at a rapid pace, and there are no signs of it slowing down. An online article from July 11, 2022, written by Tatiana Walk-Morris, titled "Report: E-commerce sales to exceed $1 trillion this year," stated, "FTI Consulting predicts online retail sales will hit the $1 trillion milestone in Q3 of 2022, a doubling from four years prior."

Online shopping is becoming more popular each year as consumers become more comfortable with making online purchases. This rise in mobile commerce is giving consumers additional options for how they want to shop.

Some key trends that will shape the future of e-commerce include personalization, as consumers will expect companies to know their personal preferences and tailor their unique shopping experience accordingly. Artificial intelligence (AI) and machine learning (ML) will play significant roles in helping businesses make sense of all the data they are collecting at every stage of the consumer journey. Moreover, virtual reality (VR) and augmented reality (AR) is becoming more widespread as retailers look for ways to give shoppers an immersive experience.

The future of business to business (B2B) selling is exciting. With the advent of new technologies, the way we sell to businesses is changing rapidly. No longer are we limited by geographical boundaries. We can now reach out to potential customers worldwide with the click of a button. What's more, the traditional sales process is being disrupted by new, more efficient methods such as inbound selling that focuses on creating relationships with clients rather than simply trying to close a deal. This approach results in higher-quality leads and a better chance of closing business deals.

Account-based marketing (ABM) is another new method that is proving to be highly effective in the B2B sales world. This approach involves targeting specific companies that are more likely to be interested in your product or service. Tailoring your marketing and sales efforts to these specific companies increases your organization's chances of success.

ABM is a strategic approach to marketing that focuses on key accounts within an organization's market. ABM is a structured process that aligns sales and marketing teams to work together to target, engage and win business with specific, named accounts.

The key benefits of ABM are:

- Improved alignment between sales and marketing teams
- More efficient use of marketing resources
- Improved focus on key accounts
- Better ROI from marketing campaigns

ABM emerged in the early 2000s in response to the rise of mass-marketing strategies. In traditional marketing, businesses would take a "spray-and-pray" approach, casting a wide net with their marketing campaigns to reach as many potential customers as possible. However, this approach was becoming increasingly ineffective as customer acquisition costs continued to rise.

In contrast, ABM aims to build relationships with key decision-makers within key accounts and create a tailor-made strategy for each. This approach is more efficient and effective than traditional marketing, allowing businesses to focus their resources on a smaller number of high-value targets.

While having its origins in direct marketing and account management, ABM has evolved to become a holistic approach that encompasses all aspects of the customer journey.

Overall, as we know, sales is a notoriously tough profession. It's demanding, high-pressure, and often thankless. But it can also be immensely rewarding. When your outcome is to create celebration rather than just creating cash, fear of rejection becomes a thing of the past. If someone refuses your invitation to join in the celebration, who is the one who really lost out? Not you. You just continue celebrating along the way.

Your Life at the Next Level

Can the mastery of sales make you rich? Without a doubt. It probably won't happen overnight (at least not legally), but sales mastery will make you rich if that's what you desire. Can the mastery of sales make you wealthy? That is a much different question. Not only can the mastery of sales make you wealthy surprisingly quickly, the fact that you've reached this stop along our journey means you are already well on your way.

Wealth is often associated with money, but the true meaning of wealth goes beyond that. Wealth is about having good health, being happy, and having a strong spirit. Money can help you get there, but it's not the only thing that matters. Your health is one of the most important things in life. If you're not healthy, you can't enjoy anything else. That's why it's so important to take care of yourself both physically and mentally. Exercise and eat healthy foods, and make sure to get enough sleep. Taking care of your body will help you stay healthy and happy.

Being happy is also important for your well-being. If you're always stressed out or unhappy, you won't be able to enjoy life to the fullest. Find things that make you happy and do them every day. On the material end of the scale, Paul Sullivan wrote a column called "Wealth Matters" for *The New York Times* for 13 years and 608 installments, speaking to an estimated 4,846 sources about wealth in America. I'd like to quote Mr. Sullivan from an online article called, "The Difference Between 'Rich' and 'Wealthy,' According *to New York Times* 'Wealth Matters' Columnist," originally published on *Grow* (CNBC + Acorns), Dec. 16, 2021, written by Ryan Ermey.

According to Mr. Sullivan, "The people that I consider wealthy—whether you're a schoolteacher or a billionaire—are the people who, when they want to do X, they can do it." I would say that is about as clear and simple an explanation of what wealth truly is from a financial standpoint as one could ask. The article goes on to say, "If your savings afford you the ability to do whatever you want to do, you are wealthy."

In a related article from *Grow*, written by Aditi Shrikant and published on July 22, 2021, titled, "A lot of people with money don't have 'wealth': A political scientist, psychologist, and CFP on what makes you 'wealthy.'" In the article, Ms. Shrikant quoted Susan Bradley, CFP®, CeFT®, who is the founder of the Sudden Money® Institute, which she started 20 years ago.

In the article, Ms. Bradley says, "Wealth to me is a much bigger, deeper experience, and a lot of people with money don't have wealth."

Mastering sales has enabled me to enjoy great wealth from quite a young and tender age, and I wish you massive wealth from this moment forward. Always Be Connecting and Always Be Celebrating.

I wish you massive wealth from this moment forward. Always Be Connecting and Always Be Celebrating.

Key Takeaways in Chapter 8

- The future of selling is digital and interactive. This trend is set and unstoppable.
- Artificial intelligence, machine learning, virtual reality, augmented reality and whatever comes next will change the world of selling in ways we have yet to imagine.
- One thing that will never change—the best way to create loyal customers is to provide them with spontaneous, unforgettable and positive life experiences.
- Find things that make you happy and do them every day. Take your life to the next level.

Chapter 9

SUGGESTED READING

Brain Scripts for Sales Success
Whitman, Drew Eric. *Brain Scripts for Sales Success*. McGraw–Hill Education, 2015.

Emotional: How Feelings Shape Our Thinking
Mlodinow, Leonard. *Emotional: How Feelings Shape Our Thinking*. Pantheon, 2022.

From Impressed to Obsessed: 12 Principles for Turning Customers and Employees into Lifelong Fans
Picoult, Jon. *From Impressed to Obsessed: 12 Principles for Turning Customers and Employees into Lifelong Fans*. McGraw Hill Professional, 2021.

The Persuasion Code: How Neuromarketing Can Help You Persuade Anyone, Anywhere, Anytime
Morin, Christophe, and Patrick Renvoisé. *The Persuasion Code: How Neuromarketing Can Help You Persuade Anyone, Anywhere, Anytime*. John Wiley & Sons, 2018.

The Science of Selling: Proven Strategies to Make Your Pitch, Influence Decisions, and Close the Deal
Hoffeld, David. *The Science of Selling: Proven Strategies to Make Your Pitch, Influence Decisions, and Close the Deal*. Penguin, 2016.

Selling Boldly: Applying the New Science of Positive Psychology to Dramatically Increase Your Confidence, Happiness, and Sales
Goldfayn, Alex. *Selling Boldly: Applying the New Science of Positive Psychology to Dramatically Increase Your Confidence, Happiness, and Sales*. John Wiley & Sons, 2018.

Sell More with Science the Mindset, Traits, and Behaviors that Create Sales Success
Hoffeld, David. *Sell More with Science the Mindset, Traits, and Behaviors that Create Sales Success*. Penguin, 2022.

What Great Salespeople Do
Bosworth, Michael T., Ben Zoldan, and Michael T. Bosworth. *What Great Salespeople Do*. McGraw-Hill Publishing, 2012.

ABOUT THE AUTHOR

Ruth M. Farrington is a sales and business operations expert with over 48 years of experience in medium to high-end retail. She has held numerous leadership positions in sales, merchandising, wholesaling, and customer service for apparel and luxury goods companies. She currently applies her expertise across online and in-store purchasing to provide a cohesive customer experience.

Ruth is a master at turning around underperforming teams and operations into local, regional, and top national performers. She has a proven track record for engineering comprehensive and successful sales and operational turnarounds at retail locations for a variety of well-known brands. Her work has resulted in billions of dollars in sales revenue throughout her career.

A native of New York for over 40 years and a proud mother of three remarkable sons, Ruth now lives in her hometown of Cleveland, Ohio, where she continues to work with and train younger sales professionals to follow in and exceed her footsteps.

A free ebook edition is available with the purchase of this book.

To claim your free ebook edition:

1. Visit MorganJamesBOGO.com
2. Sign your name CLEARLY in the space
3. Complete the form and submit a photo of the entire copyright page
4. You or your friend can download the ebook to your preferred device

Morgan James BOGO™

A **FREE** ebook edition is available for you or a friend with the purchase of this print book.

CLEARLY SIGN YOUR NAME ABOVE

Instructions to claim your free ebook edition:
1. Visit MorganJamesBOGO.com
2. Sign your name CLEARLY in the space above
3. Complete the form and submit a photo of this entire page
4. You or your friend can download the ebook to your preferred device

Print & Digital Together Forever.

Snap a photo

Free ebook

Read anywhere

Printed in the USA
CPSIA information can be obtained
at www.ICGtesting.com
JSHW080101040224
56566JS00002B/31